Timothy Shay Arthur

The Mother's Rule

The right way and the wrong way

Timothy Shay Arthur

The Mother's Rule
The right way and the wrong way

ISBN/EAN: 9783744714983

Printed in Europe, USA, Canada, Australia, Japan

Cover: Foto ©Lupo / pixelio.de

More available books at **www.hansebooks.com**

THE YOUNG MOTHER.

THE

MOTHER'S RULE;

OR,

The Right Way and the Wrong Way.

EDITED BY

T. S. ARTHUR.

NEW YORK
JOHN W. LOVELL COMPANY
150 WORTH STREET, CORNER MISSION PLACE

Copyrighted by
HUBBARD BROTHERS.
1883.

PREFACE.

As the mother's rule at home is, so, in a large measure, will be the characters of her children. By the mother is determined the future of her offspring. She may bend their natural impulses to good, or permit young life, in its first eager activities, to take on evil forms that will forever after mar the beautiful aspects of humanity. How vastly important is it, then, for mothers to have a higher regard for their duties—to feel deeply the immense responsibilities that rest upon them! It is through their ministrations that the world grows worse or better.

True words, fitly spoken, have often a wonderful power for good. Many doubting, desponding, or listless ones have been suddenly awakened to vigorous activity in the right direction, by a single vivid illustration of truth, and the good fruit, springing up in due time, has been seen of all men. True words for mothers, under various forms of narrative, poetry, and earnest teaching, have we gathered together in this volume, which is now sent forth to do its work. The good seed we are sure will find good ground, and ripe fruit appear in after time.

CONTENTS.

BE PATIENT WITH CHILDREN	Page 7
GOVERNING CHILDREN	13
DISCIPLINE	20
MY STEP-MOTHER	23
A MOTHER'S EYES	34
WHERE IS HEAVEN?	35
A CHAPTER ON TEASING	40
CHILDHOOD	45
MAY BE SO	47
ARE YOU A PARENT?	53
CHRISTMAS EVE AND CHRISTMAS MATINS	55
MANAGING CHILDREN	73
THE MOTHER'S RESOLVE	76
BE CAREFUL HOW YOU TREAT CHILDREN	98
GRANDMOTHER'S STORY	100
I DREAMED OF MY MOTHER	123
MOTHERS, DO YOU SYMPATHIZE WITH YOUR CHILDREN?	126
PASSING THROUGH THE FIRE	132
FITS OF OBSTINACY	158
THE SENSITIVE MOTHER	161
THE MOTHER'S PRAYER	179
MRS. HALE'S TWO VISITS	180
MANAGEMENT OF CHILDREN	187
THE BRIGHT SIDE	195
A WORD TO PARENTS	198

HOUSEHOLD MUSIC	201
LOVE'S YEARNING	204
DEAL GENTLY WITH THE TIMID CHILD	212
TWO IN HEAVEN	214
THE MOTHER AND THE SON	215
MOTHER	218
THE KEY TO THE HEART	221
"LITTLE THINGS"	222
THE CHILDREN AND THE NOVEL	226
A REVELATION OF CHILDHOOD	234
DISCRIMINATION WITH RESPECT TO CHILDREN	248
HOME ECONOMY	255
YOUNG MOTHER	263
HOW TO MAKE BOYS LOVE HOME	265
HAPPY AT HOME	268
OUR OLD GRANDMOTHER	269
GOVERNMENT OF CHILDREN	275
SPECIAL EDUCATION	277
FAULT-FINDING	280
THE PECUNIARY INDEPENDENCE OF CHILDREN	286
EXCITING IMAGINARY FEARS	287
CHILD-TALK	290
TEACH YOUR CHILDREN FROM THE BIBLE	293
PUNISHMENT	296
THOUGHTS FOR MOTHERS	298
HEALTH OF CHILDREN	299

THE MOTHER'S RULE.

BE PATIENT WITH CHILDREN.

"YE HAVE NEED OF PATIENCE!" Nothing can be more true than this, and nothing is more applicable to those who have to do with boys and girls. There are so many provocations which demand endurance, so many faults which require correction, so much carelessness which provokes rebuke, and so much perverseness which calls for firmness and control, that "teachers of babes," if not of a temper absolutely angelic, need to have "line upon line—line upon line, precept upon precept—precept upon precept," to aid in the work which has fallen to their lot.

There are so many temptations and accessories to impatience, too. It is so easy and so natural for the strong to tyrannize over the weak! Absolute power is too frequently abused; and the power which a parent or a teacher exercises over the child, is so far absolute that immediate resistance can be rendered unavailing. True, the parent has parental tenderness and love to restrain the impetuosity of impatience, but the teacher has not; and if parents are often, in spite of natural barriers, impetuous, what wonder that teachers are so too.

It is less trouble, so far as the present time is concerned, to blame and scold, and punish a child for negligence, stupidity, or misconduct, than to explain, reason, and instruct. It takes less time to box a boy's ears for being mischievous, or to push a girl into a bedroom "all by herself," for being idle, or talkative, or troublesome, than it does to investigate intentions and motives, or to inquire into causes; and we do not wonder that the patience of the most patient sometimes gives way. But it is not the less to be deplored when it does give way. In one hour—in less time than this—in *one minute*, evil may be wrought which will undo the work of months, or which years of judicious treatment will not obliterate.

Do we say, then, that children should be indulged and pampered, and their faults overlooked? No; this again seems easier to the indulgent and self-indulgent teacher than the wearying work of constant watchfulness and wise circumspection. But patience is as much required in the avoidance of false indulgence, as in the banishment of undue or injudicious severity. It is easier, for the moment, to yield to the wishes and dispositions of children, than to oppose or regulate them. But notwithstanding this, "Patience" should "have her perfect work." O ye teachers of the young, "ye have need of patience."

And not patience only. In the proper exercise of discipline, discrimination and keen perception must be united with it, or even patience will fail. Perhaps no two children in any given number are precisely alike in formation of mind, disposition, and general capacity. One will be timid, another bold; one sensitive, another obtuse; one quick, another slow. In different things, and at different times, the same boy or girl may exhibit almost contradictory qualities, and yet there shall be nothing in all this that ought to be construed into a fault, or that should call for even a rebuke. Patience here will be lost in a maze, to which discrimination alone can furnish the clue. And that not always, for we have the word of inspiration to assure us that "the heart is deceitful above all things;" but in general, perhaps, the heart of a child may be pretty correctly read by those who do not, idly or contemptuously, neglect its study.

At all events, it is better to be credulous than incredulous—better that a child should ten times escape the just punishment of a fault through an excess of patience, than be once unjustly punished through want of discrimination. The memory of the injustice will rankle in the soul, and produce worse fruits there, tenfold, in after years, than will spring from the consciousness of having committed faults innumerable with impunity.

Teachers or parents never will or can deal wisely with a child, unless they dispense with impulse, and scrutinise, in every possible way, what appears worthy of condemnation; and the best way to follow out this scrutiny is mentally to change places with the offender—to be a child again—to divest one's self of all but a childish judgment and capacity—to throw back one's self upon childish views and feelings—and to submit to be guided by childish reasonings; and then, after all, if there be a doubt, to give the child the benefit of that doubt.

But, O, what a deal of trouble is all this!

Very well, ——, we are not thinking about your trouble, but about the child's good. Though, as to trouble, the best way of doing anything is the least troublesome way in the end. But by trouble you mean pains-taking, time, and attention, and regard to the ultimate object. Now, can anything in the world, worth doing, be well and properly accomplished without these? Can a pudding be made, or a pig be fed, or a beard be shaven without these?

Trouble! Shame upon those who, under the selfish, but vain plea of saving themselves trouble—present trouble—make trouble for others in after years! Let them do anything, be anything, rather than teachers of the young.

This is an inexhaustible subject—the right training of children; we have written about it before, and we may have occasion to revert to it again and again. Meanwhile, as illustrative of the foregoing remarks, we quote an instructive passage from a work on "Private Education."

"How can you be so stupid?" said a governess to her pupil; "why do you not do your sum properly? It is very easy, and you don't try to do it well."

"My sum was right at first, and now I have done it ever so many times, I really cannot understand it," replied the child.

"I shall make you finish it," said the governess; "and not allow you to have any recreation till it is correct."

The child burst into tears, saying she did not know how it was, but she felt so stupid. She, however, sat down, and once more began the sum; but, this time, every figure was wrong.

The governess grew very angry, and said the naughty girl should not only begin it again, but do two more as a punishment for such obstinacy.

The child made another attempt, and was desired to do it aloud.

"Four farthings make a shilling," said the child.

"What!" exclaimed the governess; "four farthings make a shilling! How dare you be so stupid? You do it on purpose. I shall certainly complain to your mamma."

"Indeed, indeed," sobbed the child, "I will try to do it properly; I see I am wrong, very wrong; I mean to say, twelve farthings make a penny."

The governess could bear it no longer; she rose, and was about to threaten some severe punishment, when the mother entered the room, and, seeing the child in tears, said,

"What is the matter with my little Emma? Seven o'clock, and lessons not finished! I am going to dinner, and you will not be ready for dessert."

"I am not to go down stairs this evening," replied the weeping child; "I cannot do my sum."

The governess, till then silent, confirmed this—"I cannot allow Miss Emma any recreation." she said; and drawing out her watch, added, "it is now seven o'clock, she has been five hours with a slate in her hand, and has not yet done her sum. I am sorry to say she is very obstinate, and persists in asserting that four farthings make a shilling, and that twelve farthings make a penny!"

The child stared vacantly, and did not contradict her governess, but looked as if not conscious of the mistake she had made. The mother, evidently suffering at seeing her child's swollen eyes, and convinced of the mismanagement, merely said,

"I am sorry to find Emma has given cause for displeasure, and beg she may be sent to bed immediately; to-morrow, I trust, she will endeavour to be more attentive."

The child obeyed, sobbing, "Good-night, mamma."

As soon as she was gone, Mrs. Y., an excellent and judicious parent, pointed out, in gentle language, the error committed:—

"You will probably think, Miss H., that a mother's feelings mislead me; but I must candidly say, I do not think Emma has been so much to blame. You have shown ill-judged severity in keeping her so long at the same lesson. I give you credit for your good intentions, but believe me you are mistaken. The attention, fixed for such a length of time, loses its power; and I am persuaded that Emma will do her sum right to-morrow morning, provided no threats are made; but if her thoughts be occupied with the punishment she has to dread, it is not probable she can give undivided attention to any study, much less to arithmetic, which admits of no error. I do not think Emma deserved to be punished; she had no power of doing better. It is evident, from her saying that four farthings make a shilling, and twelve farthings make a penny, that she was much puzzled; and I beg that another time, under similar circumstances, she may be made to leave off her lesson. When I sent her to bed, and appeared displeased, it was to uphold your authority; I should not have had the courage to inflict any other punishment; but the child was so fatigued I thought it could do her no harm, and hope she is already asleep, as I fear she has been over-exerted."

The governess made no reply; she felt the truth of the observations, and was grateful for the manner in which they had been conveyed.

The following morning the little girl, refreshed by sleep, and recovering the use of her faculties, did her sum without a single mistake, and begged, as a reward, that she might be allowed to go and show it to her mamma.

GOVERNING CHILDREN.

"I'll not live in this way!" exclaimed Mrs. Lyon, passionately. "Such disorder, wrangling, and irregularity, rob me of all peace; and make the house a bedlam, instead of a quiet home. Tom!"—she spoke sharply to a bright little fellow, who was pounding away with a wooden hammer on a chair, and making a most intolerable din;—"stop that noise, this instant! And you. Em', not a word more from your lips. If you can't live in peace with your sister, I'll separate you. D'ye hear! Hush, this instant!"

"Then make Jule give me my pincushion. She's got it in her pocket."

"It's no such thing; I haven't," retorted Julia.

"You have, I say."

"I tell you I haven't!"

"Will you hush?" The face of Mrs. Lyon was fiery red; and she stamped upon the floor, as she spoke.

"I want my pincushion. Make Jule give me my pincushion."

Irritated, beyond control, Mrs. Lyon caught Julia by the arm; and thrusting her hand into her pocket, drew out a thimble, a piece of lace, and a penknife.

"I told you it wasn't there! Couldn't you believe me?"

This impertinence was more than the mother could endure; and, acting from her indignant impulses, she boxed the ears of Julia, soundly. Conscious, at the same time, that Emily was chiefly to blame for all this trouble, by a wrong accusation of her sister; she turned upon her, also, administering an equal punishment. Frightened by all this, the younger children, whose incessant noise, for the last hour, had contributed to the overthrow of their mother's temper, became suddenly quiet, and skulked away into corners—and the baby, that was seated on the floor, between two pillows, curved her quivering lips, and glanced fearfully up at the distorted face in which she had been used to see the love-light that made her heaven.

A deep quiet followed this burst of passion; like the hush which succeeds the storm. Alas, for the evil traces that were left behind! Alas, for the repulsive image of that mother, daguerreotyed in an instant, on the memory of her children, and never to be effaced! How many, many times, in after years, will not a sigh heave their bosoms, as that painful reflection looks out upon them from amid the dear remembrances of childhood.

A woman of good impulses, but with scarcely any self-control, was Mrs. Lyon. She loved her children, and desired their good. That they showed so little forbearance one with the other, manifested so little fraternal affection, grieved her deeply.

"My whole life is made unhappy by it!" she would often say. "What is to be done? It is dreadful to think of a family growing up in discord and disunion. Sister at variance with sister; and brother lifting his hand against brother."

As was usual after an ebullition of passion, Mrs. Lyon, deeply depressed in spirits, as well as discouraged, retired from her family to grieve and weep. Lifting the frightened baby from the floor, she drew its head tenderly against her bosom; and, leaving the nursery, sought the quiet of her own room. There, in repentance and humiliation, she recalled the stormy scene through which she had just passed; and blamed herself for yielding blindly to passion, instead of meeting the trouble among her children with a quiet discrimination.

To weeping, calmness succeeded. Still she was perplexed in mind, as well as grieved at her own want of self-control. What was to be done with her children? How were they to be governed aright? Painfully did she feel her own unfitness for the task. By this time the baby was asleep, and the mother felt something of that tranquil peace that every true mother knows, when a young babe is slumbering on her bosom. A book lay on a shelf, near where she was sitting, and Mrs. Lyon, scarcely conscious of the act, reached out her hand for the volume. She opened, without feeling any interest in its contents; but she had read only a few sentences, when this remark arrested her attention.

"All right government of children begins with self-government."

The words seemed written for her; and the truth expressed, was elevated instantly into perception. She saw it in the clearest light; and closed the book, and bowed her head in sad acknowledgment of her own errors. Thus, for some time, she had been sitting, when the murmur of voices from below grew more and more distinct, and she was soon aroused to the painful fact, that, as usual, when left alone, the children were wrangling among themselves. Various noises, as of pounding on, and throwing about chairs, and other pieces of furniture, were heard; and, at length, a loud scream, mingled with angry vociferations, smote upon her ears.

Indignation swelled instantly in the heart of Mrs. Lyon; hurriedly placing the sleeping babe in its crib, she started for the scene of disorder, moved by an impulse to punish severely the young rebels against all authority: and was half-way down the stairs, when her feet were checked by a remembrance of the sentiment—" All right government of children begins with self-government."

"Will anger subdue anger? When storm meets storm, is the tempest stilled?" These were the questions asked of herself, almost involuntarily. "This is no spirit in which to meet my children. It never has, never will enforce order and obedience," she added, as she stood upon the stairs, struggling with herself, and striving for the victory. From the nursery came louder sounds of disorder. How weak the mother felt! Yet, in this very weakness was strength.

"I must not stand idly here," she said, as a sharper cry of anger smote her ears; and so she moved on quickly, and opening the nursery door, stood revealed to her children. Julia had just raised her hand to strike Emily, who stood confronting her with a fiery face. Both were a little startled at their mother's sudden appearance; and both, expecting the storm that usually came at such times, began to assume the defiant, stubborn air with which her intemperate reproofs were always met.

A few moments did Mrs. Lyon stand looking at her children—grief, not anger upon her pale countenance. How still all became! What a look of wonder came gradually into the children's faces, as they glanced one at the other! Something of shame was next visible. And now, the mother was conscious of a new power over the young rebels of her household.

"Emily," said she, speaking mildly, yet with a touch of sorrow in her voice that she could not subdue; "I wish you would go up into my room, and sit with Mary while she sleeps."

Without a sign of opposition, or even reluctance, Emily went quietly from the nursery, in obedience to her mother's desire.

"This room is very much in disorder, Julia."

Many times had Mrs. Lyon said, under like circumstances, "Why *don't* you put things to rights?" or "I never saw such girls! If all in the room was topsy turvey, and the floor an inch thick with dirt, you'd never turn over a hand to put things in order;" or, "Go and get the broom, this minute, and sweep up the room. You're the laziest girl that ever lived." Many, many times, as we have said, had such language been addressed by Mrs. Lyon, under like circumstances, to Julia and her sisters, without producing anything better than a grumbling, partial execution of her wishes. But now, the mild intimation that the room was in disorder, produced all the effects desired. Julia went quickly about the work of restoring things to their right places; and, in a little while, order was apparent where confusion reigned before. Little Tommy, whose love of hammering was an incessant annoyance to his mother, had ceased his din on her sudden appearance, and, for a few moments, stood in expectation of a boxed ear; for a time he was puzzled to understand the new aspect of affairs. Finding that he was not under the ban, as usual, he commenced slapping a stick over the top of an old table, making a most ear-piercing noise. Instantly Julia said, in a low voice, to him,

"Don't, Tommy,—don't do that. You know it makes mother's head ache."

"Does it make your head ache, mother?" asked the child, curiously, and with a pitying tone in his voice, as he came creeping up to his mother's side, and looking at her as if in doubt whether he would be repulsed or not.

"Sometimes it does, my son," replied Mrs. Lyon, kindly; "and it is always unpleasant. Won't you try to play without making so much noise?"

"Yes, mother, I'll try," answered the little fellow, cheerfully. "But I'll forget sometimes."

He looked earnestly at his mother, as if something more was in his thoughts.

"Well, dear, what else?" said she encouragingly.

"When I forget, you'll tell me; won't you?"

"Yes, love."

"And then I'll stop. But don't scold me, mother; for then I can't stop."

Mrs. Lyon's heart was touched. She caught her breath, and bent her face down, to conceal its expression, until it rested on the silken hair of the child.

"Be a good boy, Tommy, and mother will never scold you any more;" she murmured gently, in his ears.

His arms stole upwards, and as they were twined closely about her neck, he pressed his lips tightly against her cheek—thus sealing his part of the contract with a kiss.

How sweet to the mother's taste were these first fruits of self-control! In the effort to govern herself, what a power had she acquired! In stilling the tempest of passion in her own bosom, she had poured the oil of peace over the storm-fretted hearts of her children.

Only first fruits were these. In all her after days did that mother strive with herself, ere she entered into a contest with the inherited evils of her children; and just so far as she was able to overcome evil in herself, was she able to overcome evil in them. Often, very often, did she fall back into old states; and often, very often, was self-resistance only a light effort; but the feeble influence for good that flowed from her words or actions, whenever this was so, warned her of error, and prompted a more vigorous self-control. Need it be said, that she had an abundant reward?

DISCIPLINE.

No parent, who reads the following, can fail to be impressed with the benefits of that "Discipline," the foundation of which is mildness, gentleness, and love. Those of us who have "little Marys" and "little brothers," to rear up for usefulness, may take a hint from this finely-constructed sketch, and go and do likewise.

Little Mary once struck her brother during my absence from the house. The stick in her hand had a sharp knot, which went clear through his cheek, making an ugly gash. The blood flowed in a stream, the boy screamed piteously, and Mary was exceedingly alarmed. She had no animosity against her little playmate; on the contrary, she loved him dearly, and when her mother, who was called to the room by his screams, came in, her little daughter had thrown her arms around his neck, and was joining her cries to his, while the red blood poured full in her face. When mother had made inquiries, she took the boy away to dress the wound, and the girl went up stairs without a word, and crept under the bed. There she sat and sobbed for several hours. Her mother, discovering where she had gone, said not a word to her, believing that it was best to leave her for the present alone. Her own heart was much pained to hear her dear child's grief, but she was willing to let her suffer for a while, in hopes that it might be made a lasting lesson to her.

I came in a little while before night, and learned how matters stood. It was a season to me of great interest and responsibility. Upon my own action here might depend the future conduct of this child. Her violent temper had been often checked by punishment, and she had been frequently enough told of its evil consequences. Now it had led her to a great crime, and if not at once restrained, my little daughter might grow up wicked and miserable.

I considered awhile how I should act, and having humbly asked guidance of the Father of all, I took my seat in the room where the affair had happened, and took the knotty stick in my hand. Then I called out in a kind voice, "Sister, come here to pa." She was always an obedient girl, and she instantly crept out and came down to me. Never shall I forget the expression of her countenance as she looked in my face. She had wept until her eyes were greatly inflamed, but they were dry, and in her face was a look of the most profound humility and grief that I ever saw. She walked slowly to my side and bowed her head on my knees. I said, "My daughter, some naughty person has hurt your little brother very much. His cheek is cut open, and I think there will always be a scar there as long as he lives. Will my daughter tell me who did it?" I heard a little sob, and then she whispered, "It was me." I continued, "If the stick had struck his eye, he would have been made blind." She commenced weeping. I said, "If it had struck his temple, it might have killed him." She gave a low scream, and said, "O, pa!" I continued, "Yes: the blow you struck would have killed your brother if some one had not turned it aside. There was some one in the room who saw how angry my daughter was, and when she struck the sharp knotty stick into her brother's face, he turned it aside, and saved his life. Do you know who it was?" She looked up into my face with a look of almost happiness, and said, "It was God, pa." "Yes," I continued, "no one but God could have done it. He has saved my boy's life, but how sorry He must be that any little girl can have so bad a heart as you have! God never can love the bad girl in this world or in the next."

She wept now more bitterly than before. I took her hand, and led her into the room where her brother lay asleep. His face was bound up, and it was very pale.

I asked her softly, "Is little brother alive yet?" She started as if smitten with a horrible thought, and uttered an ejaculation of grief. This awoke the boy, who, casting his eyes about, and seeing Mary bathed in tears, reached out his arms and called her. It was electric, and hardened must have been the heart which could behold this sweet reconciliation without tears.

That night, as we bowed around the sacred altar of family service, tender hearts were ours, and the angels who watched to carry our offerings upward, saw the tear-drops glittering in the fire-light, and heard low sobs as we united to ask the seal of God's approbation upon this reconciliation on earth.

MY STEP-MOTHER.

"Why, Annie! child, you have been a long time away—who have you with you? I was becoming alarmed at your long stay."

"It is Jane Benson, mother," was the reply, as Annie hurried across the room, still holding Jane's hand. "Oh, mother, Mr. Benson is going to be married, and Jane's heart is almost broken. To have a hateful step-mother! Oh, mother, is it not a pity?"

Mrs. Carleton raised herself from the sofa, and drawing Jane, who was sobbing, to her, she made her sit down beside her, and then said,

"Is this really true, Jane? Perhaps you may be mistaken."

"No, ma'am! Father told us yesterday, himself. I do wish I was dead—I am sure I shall never like her," added she, sobbing bitterly. Mrs. Carleton soothed her, and then asked if she knew the name of the lady? Jane told it, but Mrs. Carleton had never heard it before.

"But, mother, don't you pity Jane? Ought not Mr. Benson to be ashamed to marry again?" demanded Annie.

"Why, no!" said Mrs. Carleton. "Mr. Benson has undoubtedly a right to marry again, and perhaps Jane may, some of these days, be very thankful that he has done so. It all depends on the person whom he marries. If she is kind and good, I shall congratulate Jane with my whole heart, instead of being grieved for her."

"Kind and good!" echoed Annie; "why I thought all step-mothers were cross and hateful."

"Did you, Annie? I suspect you did not *think* much about it; but I am sorry to hear my daughter speak so harshly; especially as I owe to my step-mother whatever is amiable in my character."

"Yours, dear mother? Had you a step-mother? Is not grandma your own mother?"

"I could not possibly have loved my own mother more; and yet she certainly is one of the race you choose to call cross and hateful. Could I have supposed, for an instant, that you indulged in such violent prejudices, I would have tried to remove them before, but I will now tell you how mine were overcome, for I must begin by confessing that I had them to as great an extent as yourself. It may be of service to Jane, too."

"Please stop, mother, until I bring a cushion to sit on;" which being done, Annie seated herself on the floor at her mother's feet, and Jane sliding down beside her, they watched Mrs. Carleton's face with extreme interest. After a slight pause, as if to consider, she began:—

"My mother died when my brother Frank was thirteen years old. I was eleven; and then came the little Ellen, everybody's pet, who was about three years old. We were all that was left of a large family. My mother, some years before her death, secured the services of a distant connexion, who acted as a sort of housekeeper, and who went by the name of 'Cousin Sally.' As a housekeeper, she was invaluable; nothing was wasted; the house was in perfect order; our clothes were attended to, and my mother seemed to think she was highly favoured in securing, at any price, such a pattern of housekeepers.

"It was more than two years after the death of my mother, that our household was thrown in a great consternation by the arrival of two letters from my father to Cousin Sally and Frank, stating that he would be married in a week, and in a few more bring home his bride. Frank's letter was kindness itself, and it begged him to reconcile me to what was now inevitable, and to endeavour to remove prejudices from my mind that could only last until we were mutually acquainted. The one to Cousin Sally contained a wish that she should retain the same situation, but if it was disagreeable to her, an offer of a year's salary in consideration of her kindness to us. To have heard Cousin Sally, a stranger would have thought that she had intended filling my mother's place herself, but such was not the case. In her opinion we were getting along very quietly, and now a stranger was coming to make us all uncomfortable She would break out with—

"'She (the bride) could not be any great things, to come in that way into a man's house and turn all things upside down,—she only wondered where some people got their assurance; she knew that she must be a bold and forward piece, for Mr. Ross would never have thought of marrying, if some one had not put it in his head. Now, *she* would come and spoil all the comfort we had; but as Mr. Ross had said she (Cousin Sally) should do as she pleased, she meant to stay, and not let the children be cowed down by any step-mother.'

"It was in vain Frank urged that his father had spoken of his future wife's good temper. Cousin Sally said a woman would be a fool to show temper before marriage; she only hoped she would not live to see Frank change his mind—which wish did not seem to be exactly sincere.

"I listened to all that was said, as though it had been uttered by an oracle, though I did not know much about oracles in those days, and made up my mind never to like my step-mother.

"When we were alone, and Frank besought me to wait and see, I was only the more determined to dislike her, and we were a wretched set during the week that passed ere their arrival.

"How distinctly," continued Mrs. Carleton, "I remember the whole scene! It seems but the other day that we were seated in the parlour, awaiting their arrival. The lamps were lighted, and Frank sat reading, or pretending to read. Nelly sat on the floor with her doll and seemed afraid of coming in the door, by the glances she gave. I (with a face swelled from continual crying), having tried each seat in the room, had worked myself in a passion at Frank's hardness of heart. He had done all he could to soothe me, and had left me from sheer inability to propose any other plan.

"At last the door opened, and my father entered, leading in a lady. She was about middle size, plainly, but richly dressed. Frank went forward, but, though I rose, I remained standing in the same place. The lady held out her hand, and said,

"'I have the advantage, Frank! I have heard so much about you, I feel as if I had known you a long time.' It was not the words she spoke, but the manner that won Frank's heart. It said, 'I have heard nothing but what does you credit.' She appeared to be quite content with the expression of his crimsoned face, as he kissed the hand he held.

"'Annie!' said my father, but I did not move.

"'Annie's head has been so bad, all day,' said Frank, kindly.

"'My poor child,' said she; 'and you have been sitting up so late for us,' and she bent down and kissed my forehead. 'You seem quite feverish;' but, turning away, I threw myself into my father's arms and cried bitterly.

"Again and again he pressed me to him, and expressed his sorrow for my headache, while Frank was assisting his new mother to make friends with Nelly, who, after one of those scrutinizing looks that children can give, allowed herself to be taken up on her lap, and smilingly answered all questions.

"Cousin Sally was asked for, and presented; but, although she could find no fault with her reception, yet she declared it was all make believe, as she undressed me on going to bed.

"The next day my step-mother made many attempts to conciliate me, and at last proposed my showing her the house. I obeyed, of course, and when we were in my room, she seated herself, and putting her arm around me, said,

"'I am sorry, dear Annie, that you seem so unfriendly towards me. I do not wonder at your reluctance to see any one fill your mother's place, nor do I expect you to love me at once. Try, dear Annie, to look on me as a friend, who will do all in her power to make you happy. Do not give way to dislike without cause. If not for my sake, try and love me for your father's; will you not?"

"I have often wondered since, how I could have resisted her pleadings. My feelings were rapidly thawing, when Cousin Sally's speeches about the deceitfulness of step-mothers flashed across my brain, and to her evident sorrow and surprise, I turned coldly away.

"How often, since, I have wondered at her patience, and thought how much she must have loved my father, to have endured all that I made her suffer, and yet never to complain to him! Was it to be wondered at that her heart turned to Frank and Nelly, who almost adored her? Sometimes, when obliged by a strong sense of duty to curb and restrain me, I always had ample revenge in her look of regret, as I turned away, saying, 'If you were my own mother you would not do so.'

"Do not imagine, my dear children," said Mrs. Carleton, "that I really thought so—for, in general, children have a keen sense of justice; but Cousin Sally always took my part, and inwardly made use of the words—'It is easy to see you are not one of her children.' As to Frank and Nelly's going over to the enemy, as she termed it, she regarded it as a personal insult.

"Time passed on—spring had come, when Frank returned home one day, complaining of sickness and pain in his head; he threw himself on the sofa, refusing to go to bed, as he said he would be sure to imagine himself very ill. My step-mother brought pillows, and gave order that no visiters should be admitted. Frank was restless, and complained he could not find an easy position.

"'Let me sit in the corner, Frank,' said she. Putting a pillow on her lap, she gently laid his head on it, and commenced smoothing his curls with her comb.

"'Thank you! how cool your hands feel! please comb on, it feels so soothing,' said he, as he at last lay quiet and finally dropped to sleep. Nelly and I went out of the room, and, about an hour after, father came home. He seemed much surprised, and sent for the doctor, who said it might be the measles, and that a few hours would decide. My father asked if he would recommend Nelly and me to leave the house. The doctor would not hear of it. The best thing for us was to have them now as the season was favourable, and he approved of children's having them, if possible, when young. Frank was delirious all night. The doctor came early, and seemed very anxious.

"But it is useless to dwell on the details. He was dangerously ill, and my step-mother nursed him night and day. At length the doctor pronounced him out of danger, and said he only required her care. After he had gone, Frank complained that his pillows were not comfortable: my step-mother raised his head, but, not pleasing him, said,

"'Support yourself by clasping your arms round my neck. I can then have both hands free, dear Frank.'

"He did so, and, after making the desired change, instead of loosening his hold, he drew her face to his, saying,

"'You could not do more for me, if I was your own son.'

"'I certainly think I could not love you more, Frank!'

"Frank was too weak to do more than kiss the cheek he still held pressed against his own, and murmured, softly,

"'My *dear* mother!'

"Her eyes filled with tears, as she turned away; but catching a glimpse of me, as I sat crouching in the easy-chair, she said,

"'Frank! here is Annie, come to congratulate you.'

"Frank looked at me; and my step-mother, reaching her hand out to mine, drew me towards them. Frank kissed me, and holding a hand of each, he fell asleep. Softly disengaging my hand, she said gently to me,

"'Run away, dear Annie! it is too close in this room for you.'

"I suppose I must have looked more gentle than usual, for she kissed me, saying,

"'Go! my dear child.'

"For the first time in my life, I returned the kiss; and then, ashamed of having done so, looked more repelling than ever, and left the room.

"Nelly next took the measles, but she had them very lightly; my turn came next, and I was sick, indeed!

"Cousin Sally would have constituted herself my sole nurse; but my step-mother would not allow it, nursing me with the same unwearying kindness with which she had nursed Frank.

"One evening I had been asleep, and, on opening my eyes, found my father in the room, and in deep conversation with my step-mother. He was urging her to take exercise in the open air; he could see that she was suffering for the want of it, and that Cousin Sally would take all proper care of me. It was her answer that made the great impression on me that I have never forgotten, as I watched her face by the changeful light of the fire.

"My dear husband! when I married you I made a vow, as far as it was in my power, to endeavour to be a mother to your children. Now, do you think if they were mine in reality, I would intrust them, when ill, to any one, if I were able to nurse them myself? More than that, I think Annie is beginning to love me. Do you not think that is worth something more than an inconvenience? She would feel hurt if I left her now to the care of any one. We will soon have her loving us as we love her."

"'Not till you have sent Cousin Sally away,' said Frank, starting from my old hiding-place, the easy-chair. 'Father, come down in the study with me, I want to talk with you;' so saying, he drew his astonished auditor out of the room, whilst my step-mother followed them with looks of great amazement—then advancing to the bed, she bent down to see if I were awake. As I made no movement, and remained silent, she concluded I was sleeping, and resumed her seat beside the fire.

"It seemed as if a veil had been removed from my mind. For the first time I thought of her, free from prejudice, and I prayed that God would spare me, that I might love her as she deserved. Still, I gave no token of what was passing in my mind, and a false shame prevented me from saying—' Mother, I love you.'

"What passed between my father and Frank, of course, at the time, I did not know. All that was told me was, the doctor had ordered change of air, and, as my step-mother came from a Southern city, it was proposed to pay her relations a visit. We were all to go. My father would escort us there, and bring us back. It seemed to surprise them that I consented so willingly to go, as no one had any idea of the change in my feelings, and I could not venture to make any demonstration.

"My step-mother seemed radiant with happiness. She was going to her mother, and she could show her the new objects of her love. Frank and Nelly she was so fond and so proud of. My faults would be hidden with the plea of illness. Her mother, who had objected to the match on account of the children, would now see what treasures they were.

"I bore the journey very well, and behaved so well to the strangers, that when Nelly and I went to bed, my step-mother praised and thanked me. As she sat talking to us, before we all knelt down in prayer, with her arm around me, I took courage and said,

"'Mother, *you* pray to-night, and pray that I may be a comfort to you, as well as Frank and Nelly.' And she did pray aloud for me, and thanked her Heavenly Father that at last He had touched my heart, and that I would always continue, in all times, in joy and in trouble, to seek for such blessings as He alone could give. It was a very simple prayer, adapted to the wants of those for whom she prayed; but, I can safely say, that never since, has any prayer I ever heard, made a greater impression on me. From that time, I felt free to love her, and when we returned home and found that Cousin Sally had gone to see her son in another state, and that my father had, during our absence, removed all the old servants, so that there was no one to utter the remarks again, I do not think there was a more united family in the city. After the death of my father, the greatest trial I ever had, was when my once hated step-mother decided on living with Nelly, who was a widow, and to whom the board of our mother was an object.

"And now, Annie, do you pity Jane as much as you did? I advise you to wait and see the future Mrs. Benson; and you, my dear Jane, I earnestly entreat, when angry thoughts rise, and they do in every bosom, think how much pain I might have spared my mother and myself, by not giving way to prejudice."

―――•―――

A MOTHER'S EYES.

A MOTHER's eyes are magnets of the child,
To draw him up to boyhood; then, like stars,
They are put out by meteoric youth
Dimming the pure calm of their holy ray.
A mother's eyes the grown-up man forgets,
As they had never been: with knitted brow,
The goddess pilot of Ambition's sea,
Steering his bark to islands all unknown
He never reaches. Lo! in dismal wreck
Those isles are covered with the ghosts of ships
That only drift there through Oblivion's night,
Touching the shore in silence.
       In old age,
Remembrance from her portrait lifts the veil,
And then a mother's eyes look forth again,
And through the soul's dark windows gaze, like doves
New lighted from the sky, and fill it thus
With thoughts of innocence and dreams of love.

WHERE IS HEAVEN?

DURING one of those still evenings in the very heart of summer, when the twilight, deepening apace, seems to withdraw the earth from us, and to bring the heavens near, a mother and her little girl sat together by an open window, and both looked up to the sky. The lady was lost in thought; but her child counted the stars in a low, merry tone, singing "Two, six, ten, twenty, a hundred,—a hundred bright stars!—Oh, how many, many, *many!* and how bright!" until, turning to her mother, and grasping her dress to secure attention, she exclaimed, with sudden energy, "Tell me, mother, is Heaven in the stars?"

"Gently, Alice," said her mother. "In the stars? No, certainly not."

"Where is it, then?—in the sky, between the stars? Do tell me where it is. Once you said you would tell me when I was old enough to understand, and I think I can understand now."

"Come here, then;" her mother replied, holding out her arms to the little girl; "sit quietly on my lap, and I will tell you something about it; but you must be very attentive, because it is not easy for a little child to comprehend such great truths. You asked, just now, whether Heaven were in the stars. What did your father tell you, yesterday, about the stars?"

"He told me that some of them, but only just a very few, were worlds something like our world, and that they went round and round the sun, and had day and night and summer and winter. The rest, he said, were great big suns, ever so far off,—oh, so far off! nobody knew how far some of them were; and he had no doubt there were worlds going round and round those suns too, and people in the worlds, who were put there to learn what is good and true; and he supposed they were tempted to do wrong, and were sometimes unhappy, as we are."

"Then, do you suppose Heaven is there?"

"Oh no! of course it is not. I did not think of that!"

"No, my darling child, Heaven is not in any place which we can see with our bodily eyes. We cannot point with hands of flesh to the road that leads to that country, nor walk along it with these feet. If you went up into the depths of the sky, and searched it through, from north to south, and from east to west, you would not find Heaven there, nor meet one angel on your way."

"Then, mother, are you sure there is a Heaven, if it is not anywhere?"

"Sure? Yes, as sure as that I love you, and that you love me. Do you love me?"

"Why, mother, you know I do!"

"Are you sure? Can you see your love?"

"No."

"Can you lay hold of it with your hands?"

"No."

"What shape is it, round or square?"

"I don't know," said Alice, laughing. "It is not any shape."

"Where is it?—can you tell me that?"

"No, I am sure I cannot. It is all inside of me; all inside my soul."

"Then you see there can be a real thing which you cannot look at with your bodily eyes, nor touch with these little hands, and which does not occupy any earthly space, but which is still a real, true, living thing. Just such a real, true thing is Heaven; only it is a different kind of a thing, different kind of world from this earth, and, like your love, does not fill natural space. You say your love is inside your soul; there, then, and not on the earth, or among the stars, which lie all outside of it, you must look for the path that leads to Heaven. If you pray to God, and try to do what you know is pleasing in His sight, He will show it to you, and lead you safely along it."

"Will He really show it to me? and will it be beautiful, all covered with flowers?"

"You know I told you we cannot see those things with our bodily eyes; but if you try to be a good girl, God will put true thoughts, and gentle, loving feelings into your heart, and they will guide you to Heaven, where the pure and happy angels live."

'Could I see the angels with my eyes?"

"Not with those eyes."

"But I have not got any other eyes."

"Yes, you have. Your spirit has eyes."

"I don't think it has, mother, for, when I shut these two up so," said Alice, pressing her lids so tightly together, that scarcely more than the tips of her long lashes were visible, "I cannot see one bit; it is all dark."

"That is because your spiritual eyes are closed."

"But why can I not open them?"

"God has not given us the power to open them while we are in this world; and, if they were open, we could no more see earthly things with them, than we can see heavenly things with our bodily eyes."

"What should I see with them?"

"Any spiritual thing that was near to you. Very painful and ugly things, if you were naughty; beautiful things, and angels, if you were good. Do you not remember, how often, in the Bible, we are told of good men who had *their eyes opened*, and saw, and talked with angels?"

"Yes," replied the little girl, and added, in a low and reverent voice, "They saw the Lord, too, after He had risen; and He blessed them. He said 'Peace be with you.'"

"Yes, love. All those holy things men saw with their spiritual eyes, when it pleased God to open them."

"Why will He not open ours now, and let us see angels?"

"God loves us, my child, with an infinite love, and if it were good for us He would; but He does not, and therefore we may know that it would do us harm. Do you think, if you saw angels and other spiritual things about you all the time, you could attend properly to your lessons, and the other duties you have to perform here?"

"No," said Alice, "I do not think I could, for even the little birds flying past make me look up from my book."

After a long pause, during which her mother kept silence, that the little one might have time to garner in her golden harvest of new thoughts, she looked up again, and said with great earnestness, "Mother, I should like to die."

Kissing tenderly the little upraised face, her mother replied, "I hope, dear one, that you *will* like to die, when it is God's will to take you; but, remember, merely dying does not take us to Heaven. You must be glad and grateful to live; you must make the very best use you possibly can of the time God gives you, for it is only so that we can become good and happy in this world, or any world. And now, my darling, it is late, and you must go to bed. Give me one more kiss; and do not forget to say your prayers before you go to sleep. If you are a good girl, I will tell you more about Heaven some other day. Good-night."

Little Alice went to bed full of thought; but no sooner had her innocent head touched the pillow, than she was in a sound, sweet sleep.

A CHAPTER ON TEASING.

"Mother," said George Manson, "may I go with the boys and skate on the great pond this evening?"

"No, George; I do not like to have you go this evening."

"Now, mother, do let me go; it will be such a fine evening, and the boys all want me to come."

"I do not think it best for you to go, George."

"Why not, mother; why can't I go?"

"You have a hard cold, and perhaps if you go, it will make you so sick you will be unable to attend school for several days."

"Oh, no, it won't make me sick, mother; I am sure it will not. My cold is not bad now, and it will be such a beautiful evening; do let me go, mother, do; won't you?"

"I am afraid, my son, that the pond is not frozen over hard enough."

"Yes, mother, it is. Only think what cold nights we have had; besides, James Edwards is going, and his father never lets him go when the ice is thin. Won't you let me go, mother?"

"You had better wait till to-morrow night."

"But the boys are all going this evening, and perhaps they will not go to-morrow night. Now, mother, only say yes, to-night, and I will not ask you again this week."

"Was there ever such a teaser! Do go; for I am

sure you will tease my life away if you stay at home, but do not complain if it makes you sick."

The next noon, Mrs. Manson's eldest daughter came to ask her mother's permission to visit one of her young friends. "Susan asked me to come this afternoon," said Mary; "may I go?"

"No, you cannot go," said Mrs. Manson, as she sent her away with a frown.

Now Mary was a girl of delicate feelings. She was by no means so fond of teasing as her mother supposed. On the present occasion, as often before, she had quite a struggle with herself, as to the course she should pursue. On the one hand, she shrank from the task of obtaining a reluctant consent from her mother by teasing; on the other hand, she very much wished to visit her friend, and had reason to think, from past experience, that she might obtain consent by means which had so often proved successful. In the present instance, her mother, who had half repented of refusing a request which, on reflection, did not appear unreasonable, was easily persuaded to withdraw her refusal, and give the desired permission.

A few days after this, Mrs. Manson paid a visit to her friend, Mrs. Day. "Mother," said Henry Day, when he returned from school at night, "Edward Smith asked me to come and see him next Saturday; may I go?"

"No, my son, you have been there very recently; I do not think it best for you to go again so soon."

"May I go out and slide with the boys till tea time?"

"Yes, my dear, you may go."

"Mother," said Emma, "Cousin Sarah wishes me to

spend the afternoon with her next Saturday; may I go?"

"Next Saturday, my daughter, is some days ahead. I cannot decide now; but come to me Saturday noon, and I will let you know. I shall be happy to gratify you if it is best for you to go; but if anything should occur to prevent, I hope my daughter will bear the disappointment cheerfully."

When the children had left the room, Mrs. Manson exclaimed, "I wish my children were like yours, Mrs. Day. Do tell me if your children never tease. My children wear me out teasing, from morning till night. If my George had been in your Henry's place, he would have given me no rest from now till Saturday noon, if I had refused to let him go."

"My children," said Mrs. Day, "never tease; and pardon me, my dear friend, if I say that when I see teasing children, I always attribute the habit entirely to the parents, regarding it as the natural effect of causes which they have set in operation."

"I cannot agree with you. I think there is a great difference in children. Some are the natural teasers. I believe my children love to tease."

"Again I must differ from you. I do not believe there is a child in the world who loves to tease. I think teasing, itself, is naturally disagreeable to every child."

"Well, I certainly know that if teasing was disagreeable to my children, they would not follow it so incessantly as they do."

"I am by no means sure of that. We all often consent to do disagreeable things, if by that means we can secure some favourite object. My own experience has convinced me that teasing is nearly or quite as disagreeable to the teaser as to the teased. When I was a child, I had the reputation of being a great teaser; but I can well recollect the reluctance with which I set about the task of procuring my mother's consent to some favourite scheme by this means. Like all children, I greatly desired the indulgence which I sought to obtain, and I had found by trial that my point was often obtained in this way, and seldom in any other. Depend upon it, no child will ever tease who has not been in the habit of gaining something by it. Children will not work so hard for nothing."

"I do not believe it would be possible to keep my children from teasing. The other evening George was bent upon going with the boys to skate upon the pond. I did not like to have him go, as he had a bad cold, but he teased every moment, till he obtained my consent."

"And can you think it strange if the next time he wishes to gain your consent to his plans, he remembers the circumstances, and is encouraged to try again? Henry would like very much to visit his friend next Saturday; but he is perfectly aware that, with his parents, NO means NO; and that no importunity changes NO to YES; and he does not think of making the attempt."

"But sometimes I refuse my children, when afterwards I am sorry I did so. What can one do, in such a case?"

"I think, my friend, we should be very careful never inconsistently to refuse our children's requests. We should remember that our decision, when once expressed, ought to be, like the laws of the Medes and Persians, unchangeable, and therefore we should not allow ourselves to be hasty in making known a decision which cannot be repealed without serious injury to the child. If it is evident that the request is reasonable, we should always grant it with cheerful promptness. This will gain the confidence of our children. They will come openly and frankly with their requests, assured that we shall not refuse them from mere caprice, and afterwards yield to their importunity."

" But if you have inconsistently refused them a reasonable request, may you never change your decision?"

" I think not. It will be better for them to abide by it, while you learn the lesson to be more careful in future."

"But suppose you cannot make up your mind, at once?"

" Then name some future time when you will let them know your decision, and let it be understood that nothing further is to be said to you on the subject till the time arrives. Pursue this course with decision and perseverance, and you may be assured that your children will quit a habit which they find not only disagreeable, but unprofitable. It greatly promotes the happiness of our children to meet their requests in this prompt and decided manner. You never saw a child in the act of teasing, whose countenance did not express more or less of a restless anxiety. He may gain his point by importunity, and he may not; and in this way the mind is often kept on the rack of suspense for hours, to the serious injury of the temper and disposition of the child."

CHILDHOOD.

Be kind to the little child. You cannot tell how one harsh word or unkind look will chill his heart, and fill his eyes with tears. You may forget that the word has been spoken, and endeavour by kind acts to win the child's affections, but you may never be able to remove the impression which that look and word have made. Many people suppose that children are less observing than older persons, and they use language before them which they would consider too "impolite" to be used before their friends and acquaintances. This is a sad and fatal mistake. A child's impressions are sometimes so lasting, that a whole lifetime's after experience is not able to remove them. Each one may recall some of the feelings of childhood, which have continued to the present time, and which a sober judgment has not been able to remove. Let the words spoken to young children be gentle, loving words, which we should not regret to have them remember in after years. Let the child be treated with sincerity, and let only the words of truth be addressed to him, for in this way alone can he be taught to practise the truth in word and action. If a slight deception is detected by a child, he will not again trust you. No effort of yours can restore that perfect confidence, which is one of the most attractive attributes of childhood. Unkindness is indeed an injury to the child, for it chills his warm affections, and teaches him to feel misery, when God meant he should be happy. But harshness is far better than deception, for this robs the soul of its trust, and may rob it of its most precious jewel, the diamond truth.

We have read of a father who once promised his son that he should be present at the blasting of a stone wall, which was to take place at a certain time. The boy was absent at the time, and the father, forgetting that he had made the promise, allowed the blasting to take place in his son's absence. The boy returned, and found that his father had broken his plighted word. For the first time in his life, his father had deceived him, and full of injured feeling, his breast swelling with disappointed hopes, he sought his father, and eagerly reminded him of his promise.

For a moment the parent's brow was overcast. He had forgotten his promise; the heavy stone wall, with great labour and expense, had been destroyed, and his son had not witnessed its destruction. But what was labour and expense compared to a father's truth? Turning to the boy, he said, "I did promise you that you should see the blasting, my son; and you shall see it. The wall shall be rebuilt, and my promise shall be performed." Accordingly the wall was rebuilt, and the boy learned that his father valued his word above all price, and would spare no expense to keep a promise which he had made his son. There are no lectures or essays which this father could have spoken which would have impressed the value of truth upon his son's mind as powerfully as did this single action.

The sorrows of childhood are often called fleeting. They are so. In most children the smile may be easily called up in the midst of tears, and the sunshine and

KIND TO THE CHILD.

clouds succeed each other very rapidly upon the face of childhood. Yet, though transient, the child's sorrows are real sorrows; and his little heart aches as truly as if years had taught him more patience. He has less philosophy, and has not yet learned to reason about his grief, nor does he realize that the darkest night is often just before day. For this very reason, he feels his sorrow more keenly than if he were older and more philosophical; and sympathy in his griefs will be as sweet to him as to one in the prime of life.

Then let the child receive sympathy in his sorrows, and let us do all in our power to lighten his grief, and soothe his pain, remembering that "Of such is the kingdom of Heaven."

MAY BE SO.

"NEXT time you go out, you'll buy me a wagon, won't you, mother?" said my little boy to me one day.

I didn't want to say "No," and destroy his happy feelings, and I was not prepared to say "yes;" and so I gave the evasive reply so often used under such circumstances, "May be so," and which was meant rather as a negative than an affirmative. The child was satisfied; for he gave my words the meaning he wished them to have. In a little while after, I had forgotten all about it. Not so my boy. To him the "may be so" was "yes;" and he set his heart confidently on receiving the wagon the next time I should go out. This happened to be on the afternoon of that very day. It was towards evening when I returned. The moment I rung the bell at my own door, I heard his pattering feet and gleeful voice in the entry.

"Where's my wagon?" said he, as I entered, a shade of disappointment falling suddenly upon his excited, happy face.

"What wagon, dear?" I asked.

"My wagon. The wagon you promised to buy me."

"I didn't promise to buy a wagon, my son."

"Oh, yes, you did, mother! You promised me this morning."

Tears were already in his eye, and his face wore a look of distressing disappointment.

"I promised to buy you a wagon? I am sure I remember nothing about it," I replied confidently. "What in the world put that into your head?"

"Didn't I ask you?" said the child, the tears now overflowing his cheeks.

"Yes, I believe you did ask me something about a wagon; but I didn't promise to buy you one."

"Oh, yes you did, mother. You said May be so."

"But 'may be so' doesn't mean yes."

At this the little fellow uttered a distressing cry. His heart was almost broken by disappointment. He had interpreted my words according to his own wishes, and not according to their real meaning.

Unprepared for an occurrence of this kind, I was not in the mood to sympathize with my child fully. To be met thus, at the moment of my return home, disturbed me.

"I didn't promise to buy you a wagon; and you must

stop crying about it," said I, seeing that he had given way to his feelings and was crying in a loud voice.

But he cried on. I went up stairs to lay off my things, and he followed, still crying.

"You must hush now," said I more positively. "I cannot permit this. I never promised to buy you a wagon."

"You said may be so," sobbed the child.

"May be so, and yes, are two different things. If I had said that I would buy you a wagon, then there would have been some reason in your disappointment; but I said no such thing."

He had paused to listen; but, as I ceased speaking, his crying was renewed.

"You must stop this now. There is no use in it, and I will not have it," said I resolutely.

My boy choked down for a few moments at this, and half stifled his grief; but overmastering him, it flowed on again as wildly as ever. I felt impatient.

"Stop this moment, I say!" And I took hold of his arm firmly. My will is strong, and when a little excited it often leads me beyond where I would go in moments of reflection. My boy knew this by experience. By my manner of speaking he saw that I was in earnest, and that, if he did not obey me, punishment would follow. So, with what must have been a powerful effort for one so young, he stifled the utterance of his grief. But the storm within raged none the less violently, and I could see his little frame quiver as he strove to repress the rising sobs.

Turning away from me, he went and sat down on a

low seat in a corner of the room. I saw his form in the glass as I stood before it to arrange my hair, after laying aside my bonnet; and for the first time my feelings were touched. There was an abandonment in his whole attitude; an air of grief about him that affected me with pity and tenderness.

"Poor child!" I sighed. "His heart is almost broken. I ought to have said yes or no; and then all would have been settled."

"Come," said I, after a few moments, reaching my hand towards the child; "let us go down and look out for father. He will be home soon."

I spoke kindly and cheerfully. But he neither moved, looked up, nor gave the smallest sign that he heard me.

"Oh, well," said I with some impatience in my voice, "it doesn't matter at all. If you'd rather sit there than come down into the parlour and look out for dear father, you can please yourself."

And turning away as I spoke, I left the chamber, and went down stairs. Seating myself at a window, I looked forth, and endeavoured to feel unconcerned and cheerful. But this was beyond my power. I saw nothing but the form of my grieving child, and could think of nothing but his sorrow and disappointment.

"Nancy," said I to one of my domestics, who happened to come into the parlour to ask me some question, "I wish you would run down to the toy store in the next block, and buy Neddy a wagon. His heart is a'most broken about one."

The girl, always willing when kindly spoken to, ran

off to obey my wishes, and in a little while came back with the article wanted.

"Now," said I, "go up into my room, and tell Neddy that I've got something for him. Don't mention the wagon; I want to take him by surprise."

Nancy went bounding up the stairs, and I placed the wagon in the centre of the room, where it would meet the child's eyes on the moment of his entrance; and then sat down to await his coming and enjoy his surprise and delight.

After the lapse of about a minute, I heard Nancy coming down slowly.

"Neddy's asleep," said she, looking in at the door.

"Asleep!" I felt greatly disappointed.

"Yes, ma'am. He was on the floor asleep. I took him up and laid him in your bed."

"Then he's over his troubles," said I, attempting to find a relief for my feelings in this utterance. But no such relief came.

Taking the wagon in my hand, I went up to the chamber where he lay, and bent over him. The signs of grief were still upon his innocent face, and every now and then a faint sigh or sob gave evidence that even sleep had not yet hushed, entirely, the storm which had swept over him.

"Neddy!" I spoke to him in a voice of tenderness, hoping that my words might reach his ear. "Neddy, dear, I've bought you a wagon."

But his senses were locked. Taking him up, I undressed him, and then, after kissing his lips, brow, and cheeks, laid him in his little bed, and placed the wagon on the pillow beside him.

Even until the late hour at which I retired on that evening, were my feelings oppressed by the incident I have described. My "May be so," uttered in order to avoid giving the direct answer my child wanted, had occasioned him far more pain than a positive refusal of his request could have done.

"I will be more careful in future," said I, as I lay thinking about the occurrence, "how I create false hopes. My yea shall be yea, and my nay, nay. Of these, cometh not evil."

In the morning when I awoke, I found Neddy in possession of his wagon. He was running with it around the room, as happy as if a tear had never been upon his cheek. I looked at him for many minutes without speaking. At last, seeing that I was awake, he bounded up to the bedside, and, kissing me, said,

"Thank you, dear mother, for buying me this wagon! You are a good mother!"

I must own to having felt some doubts on the subject of Neddy's compliment, at the time. Since this little experience, I have been more careful how I answer the petitions of my children; and avoid the "May be so," "I'll see about it," and other such evasive answers that come so readily to the lips. The good result I have experienced in many instances.

ARE YOU A PARENT?

And if so, what lessons are you teaching that child who is so fondly looking to you for guidance, who is listening to catch the first syllable that falls from your lips, and who is ready to copy the first example you may unconsciously present? Perhaps in the arms of the mother there reposes the first and only one. It is yet innocent; within its little bosom a heart beats gently, but it is a heart uncontaminated by sin, and undisturbed by care. It knows nothing of the conflicting elements of this wicked world, and as the mother gazes upon its sinless form, she firmly resolves, and the father assents, that the lessons of temperance, morality, and truth, shall early and faithfully be instilled into its young heart, and that no effort shall be wanting to rear it for usefulness to society and the world.

A few years pass away, but during this time the mind of that child has not been inactive. It has been allowed to mingle with others of its age; its range of observation has been growing wider and still wider since it left the arms of its mother; its busy feet have been active to over-step a *little* the limits which have been carefully assigned it. A second and third child have since been given, and the cares and anxieties of the parents consequently increased. There are three, now, instead of one, over which parental guardianship is to be exercised, and perhaps the business and cares of life have increased three fold in other respects. Now neglect begins to show itself, and the sad effect of this neglect is too soon apparent in the oldest child; and his influence upon the younger children is of a depressing, rather than an elevating character. Parental neglect opens the way for evil influence from another source. The child seeks companionship, and too frequently finds, in grown up persons, of vicious inclinations and habits, teachers, whose instruction is of the most fatal character. To all parents let us say :—Beware lest others corrupt the trusting hearts of your children, and lead them away from the paths of rectitude; lest others sow tares among the wheat of innocence and virtue. The unoccupied minds of your children are fields in which duty calls you to labour; and if you omit to teach them the great lessons of self-denial, if you fail to impress upon their minds and hearts a supreme regard for *truth* and *virtue*, you commit them to the boisterous ocean of life without a rudder, liable to be wrecked at every gale. We urge it as a duty incumbent on parents to give their children "line upon line, precept upon precept;" not continuing for a month nor a year only, but until mature age removes them from parental guardianship. Thus you will discharge a duty which, if faithfully attended to, will insure you the lasting gratitude and respect of your offspring, who will "rise up and call you blessed."

CHRISTMAS EVE AND CHRISTMAS MATINS.

A LITTLE cottage stood in a dark pine wood. It was a wild December evening, and the snow fell in large flakes on the low roof, and on the forest around. Light, however, shone from its little window, and lighted up the pine-trees which stretched forth their snow-laden branches towards the casement, and lit up the dismal wood outside, where the wolf sat and cried, hu, hu, hu!

The fire blazed merrily within the little one-roomed cottage, and merrily curled the blue smoke as it rose from the chimney, and fire sparks danced about with the snow-flakes which giddily tumbled down the chimney into the pan of meal porridge which stood and muttered over the fire, and thus they first tasted of the Christmas entertainment. For it was Christmas porridge which now stood and boiled on the hearth; and this was no other than Christmas eve, and at this very time, food was preparing for the whole of the holidays. It was not food for the rich man's table, of that you may be sure; it was only for a peasant woman, and she a widow, who, with her children, lived here. Nevertheless, she was about to celebrate Christmas in the best way she could, and that was not to be despised, either. She had bought for herself three pounds of meat, and this was now boiling famously with parsley and celery, and promising to make the most savory soup, together with some delicious cabbage for Christmas day. A piece of stock-fish also was lying in its pan, and was all in an agitation, as if from delight of its own excellence.

On the table in the cottage there already stood the Christmas cake, and the Christmas goblin,* that wonderful beast which seems to say, "If you come here I will gore you with my long, long horn!"

And thus would the Christmas goblin stand through the whole of the Christmas holidays, and make a great show among the Christmas meats, and then, when this festival time was over, it would be laid, together with the Christmas cake, in a chest where it would repose until spring came, and the ploughing began, and then they would take it and chop it to pieces, because the Christmas goblin is a hard piece of clay, and give it to the beasts of burden, to the oxen and horses, which have to work in the fields, and which, it was believed, would derive from this Christmas cake and goblin, such strength, and such an inclination for labour, as nobody can believe. Hence there would be abundant crops in the barns, a deal of grist for the mill, and plenty of bread in the cupboard; and all this would be caused by the Christmas goblin—that wonderful beast!

Two children, a girl and a boy, jumped about the room, and could hardly contain their joy on account of Christmas eve, and the Christmas goblin, and the Christmas meats which were cooking on the hearth, which filled the whole room with their delicious odour, and on account

* The Christmas *kuse*, which, for lack of a better word, I translate *goblin*, does not represent an evil spirit, but is merely the rude figure of some domestic animal, covered with plaited or twisted straw.

of the Christmas matins, at which they were to be pre sent with their mother. Brother Peter was to drive them in the sledge with Polle; the children had never yet been out to Christmas matins, and could not imagine what they were like, but they had heard that they were something very grand and beautiful, and they were quite sure that they were so, and moreover, that they were prodigiously amusing.

Peter, however, stood cutting firewood for baking, and thought to himself that they were not at all amusing. The mother stood just by the hearth, and busy. Why did she stand so close to the hearth, and turn her face from the happy children? The flames on the hearth saw why: they saw that her countenance was not happy, and that there were tears upon her cheeks. Why did she turn her face away from the children? Because she would not cast a shade on their happiness. She could not help it, however; she could not help thinking of her husband, who died two months before, and how happy she was last Christmas, when he was alive, and how kind he was, and how he comforted her in his last moments, and said, that if it were necessary that either husband or wife must be removed by death, how much better it was that it should be the husband, because the wife could look after the children so much better than he could.

The wife, however, now felt her lot to be a very heavy one, and had many an anxiety for the future, and most of all on account of the eldest son, her step-son Peter, who hitherto had been out at service, but who had now come home, since the father's death, to help the mother in performing the village service.* And now, precisely this very evening, when the mother had resolved for the sake of the sacred time, and for the sake of the children, to put away all anxious thoughts, precisely now have they all come thick upon her, as thick and unceasing as the snow-flakes, and when she shook them off, behold! there they were again the next moment, and made her heart so heavy—so very heavy! It was, as it were, under an evil spell.

But the children, little Erik and Maja, they could think about nothing that was gloomy.

"Nay, only look at the goblin, Maja! See how he glares at you with his big eyes! Take care! he will gore you if you only touch him. He says, 'If you come here I will run you through with my long, long horn!'"

"Nay, do you believe that he will gore me? Do you really believe that he is alive? Ah, how good that meat smells! Will it soon be ready, mother? May we soon go to Cowslip, and tell her that it is Christmas eve, and look at the stars?"†

Yes, the supper was now quite ready. The mother lighted a candle in the lanthorn, and around the candle she put a grand paper star, which the candle lit up, and

---

* The *torpare*, or cottager of Sweden, is bound to d⟩ a certain quantity of work for his landlord, in return for the small portion of land which he holds from him.

† These are Swedish peasant customs: they tell the cows and other animals, that Christmas is come, and passing a light before their eyes, see, as they fancy, the star which indicated the house in which the Saviour lay.

which, in its turn, lit up the candle. The children then took each their bread-cake, and the mother filled a jug of new brewed Christmas ale, and with the lanthorn in her hand, went out to the stable-yard to let the creatures know that it was Christmas.

The demure Mrs. Cowslip, the cow, was thinking about nothing; she was standing in her stall, chewing her cud, as the door opened, and a light flashed into her eyes. She turned towards that side, and made a low moaning, in token that she recognised those who had entered, and that they were welcome. But when the children in their zeal sprang forward, and gave her pieces of their bread, and screamed into both her ears, "It is now Christmas, Cowslip!" she stepped hastily backwards, shook her head violently, and stared as if she would say, "Nay, but that is something out of the common way!" and looked quite confounded.

But as Cowslip was a very rational and intelligent cow, she soon collected her faculties, extended her nose, smelt at her bread, took it into her mouth, and chewed it with an excellent relish, supped up a good draught of Christmas ale, and appeared quite satisfied with Christmas. When the mother had strown her a bed of fresh straw, and given her an armful of the very best and finest hay from the rack, she said, " God keep thee now, my darling; thou now hast had Christmas eve!" At these words, Cowslip seemed rightly to comprehend the matter, and with a great fragrant lock of hay in her mouth, she laid herself easily down again, that she might the better reflect, upon which she stared at the light, and had her own musings about the stars, which the children tried to make her observant of. But the only reply she made was by a gentle lowing. After that they carried the light to the stable, that it might shine upon Polle, and that they might give him a taste of Christmas bread, and announce to him that it was now Christmas.

Polle pointed his ears, and lifted his head; expanded his nostrils, and neighed with animation, as if he wished to make it known that he expected this intelligence, and that it was welcome to him.

The sheep bleated, and licked the hands that gave them their Christmas entertainment. It was so good, so very good!

As for the two little pigs, they were quite out of their senses when their turn came; they leaped about, screeched, and tumbled one over the other, so that nothing rational could be done with them. They were regularly crazy with joy.

After this the mother and her children returned to the cottage. The son, Peter, was also there. He was a tall youth of sixteen, with a dark and strongly-marked countenance. The mother cast an anxious glance upon him. Since she had come into the family, she had had a deal of trouble with his obstinate and discontented temper, which appeared to have become worse since his father's death.

And this evening, when the mother had desired him to chop wood for Christmas, he had replied, "I must do everything!" and, as he went out, he banged the door with such violence, that the earthenware cups and dishes upon the shelf jing'ed and shook a long time afterwards.

That answer grieved the mother, who well knew that she never spared herself, and never required much from him.

He now sat down with his arms propped on the table, and never seemed to observe that the mother was setting out the supper, and that she had done everything so well.

But when they were all seated at the table, and the mother had poured out the Christmas ale, the little ones glanced at each other, and then at their mother with a roguish look that seemed to say, "Now it is coming!"

And with that the mother lifted her glass, and the little ones their wooden mugs, and all three at once exclaimed,

"Your health, Peter!"

Peter looked up, and seemed almost as much astonished as Cowslip herself, when they told her that it war Christmas.

"And all happiness to you on your birthday, for upon this evening you were born," added the mother.

To which Peter replied, with a look of displeasure, "That is nothing to drink one's health about, or to wish one luck about, either! It would have been better to have been unborn!"

"That is a sinful word, my son," replied the mother, severely. "When God gives health and strength to bear, to strive, and to work——"

"Nay, but why must one strive and work?" interrupted Peter.

"My dear lad, what questions you ask!" said the mother; "must not people live?"

"And why must they live?" asked Peter, again.

The mother could not instantly find an answer to this question; it distressed her; but the lad often made use of such expressions as left a great weight upon her mind; and as she was now silent, Peter continued:—

"When one has neither father nor mother, nor any in the world to live for, it would be just as well if one were dead; then one should be rid of all one's trouble."

"Am I not your mother, Peter?" said the mother, and tears started to her eyes.

"You are only my step-mother!" said Peter, immovably, and rose up from the table.

This wounded the mother more than anything else, because she knew in her own mind that her heart had always been full of tenderness and maternal affection towards her step-son, and that she did not deserve this unkindness from him.

But she could not say anything now, nor look vexed, because it was Christmas eve.

The little ones did not understand what was amiss with their brother. Their mouths were waiting for the good soup, and they could not imagine that any one could be better off than they were. When the mother saw that their appetites were somewhat appeased, she proposed that they should put aside a portion of their supper for old Alle, in the poor-house, which delighted them, and therefore the mother tied up a part of their meat, and of their bread-cakes, in a clean blue handkerchief, and set it on a shelf till the next morning, when they should take it with them when they went out for Christmas matins. Peter, however, contributed nothing; his countenance was sullen, and before long he rose from the table, and went to bed without saying "good-night."

The little ones, also, soon lay side by side, on a large sheaf of golden straw, which they had brought in for Christmas, because, according to popular belief, people must both sleep and dance upon straw at Christmas, if they would do right.

The children did not undress themselves, that they might be ready all the sooner next morning, when they would be called for the Christmas matins. Each took a white handkerchief, which they laid under their heads, and thus fell asleep, side by side, while the firelight flickered upon them, and kissed their very cheeks, which shone out quite beautifully upon the golden-coloured wheat straw.

Last of all, the mother also went to bed, but not until she had set everything in order in the room, and washed up the dishes.

But though she now lay in bed, she could not sleep, because she had uneasy thoughts, and she heard how Peter turned and seemed uneasy in his bed, as if he could not sleep either. At one time she thought that he wept, and she considered with herself, "should I now get up and go to him, and give him a quiet kiss, he would then, perhaps, understand that I love him, although I am not his real mother; and more particularly, as it is Christmas eve, and everybody ought to part friends."

Presently, Peter seemed to be quite still, and then she thought, "he is gone to sleep, and I should only disturb him." She therefore lay quiet herself, and turned her thoughts to God, and prayed him to change the unhappy temper of the youth. She prayed for a blessing on him, and on the beloved little ones. With that, she turned round to look at them, and to see how the firelight flickered over, and kissed their rosy countenances, for the fire burned in the hearth through the Christmas night. And then she thought about all the animals, how they had their Christmas provender, and how comfortable they were; and the thoughts of them did her good, and whilst she was thinking of them, and gazing at her little ones by the firelight, she went to sleep herself.

When she again woke, it was pitch-dark in the room, and quite cold; and she felt a great weight on her heart, and in her head also. It was as if a large, heavy tear had collected, and could not find vent, but lay there as heavy as lead. She thought upon the death of her husband, upon the bitter temper of her son, and how solitary she herself was in the world; and then Peter's words occurred to her, "why should people live?" and she felt as if she would gladly not rise, but be quiet for ever.

Spite of all this, however, she rose, and lighted the fire as usual, and set on the coffee, for although she was not one of those extravagant women who drink coffee every day, yet now at Christmas time, everybody must have coffee; the whole household must drink coffee; that was a matter of course.

She then lighted the candle in the Christmas-tree by the window, which she had made ready the evening before, for the children, and that done, she woke them.

"Christmas matins, children! Christmas matins!"

The little ones started up, quite bewildered; rubbed their eyes, opened them with an effort, saw the light burning in the pine-tree, and then it came to their remembrance that it was Christmas, and that they were going to morning service. And with that they leapt up, and were quite wakeful.

They all drank their coffee, Peter as well as the rest, and then Peter, who, as usual, was silent and out of humour, went to put Polle in the sledge.

When the mother came out of the cottage, dressed in her holiday attire, with her hymn book in her hand, and two little ones at her side, she saw the moon and the morning star, standing brightly above the pine wood, and shining beautifully in the frosty early morning, and upon the new-fallen snow. The sight did her heart good.

"How beautifully," thought she, "after all, has God made every thing for mankind." She inhaled the fresh, cold, but not very cold, winter air, and felt her spirits enlivened by so doing.

Polle was in the most cheerful humour. He neighed, and pointed his ears, and tossed his handsome head, and pawed the sward with his foot, and was quite impatient to be off.

Before long, the widow sat with her two little ones in the sledge, and Peter stood between them and drove. Polle's bells jingled merrily as they sped along through wood and meadow; the morning star shone upon the white, snowy fields, and the grim wood. It was a beautiful and a cheering sight.

The little ones were full of talk.

"Nay, look!—nay, look. There's a light burning at Storgal, a light in her opposite window! And look! old Britta on the hill has got a light too! And look there, a long, long way off in the wood, there shines a light! And look, look! Nay, that is the very best of all,—those candles in the window at the gate-house. See, it is lighted the whole way! Nay, how grand it is! Is it ever grander than this at Christmas matins, mother?"

"You are two little simpletons!" said the mother. "Christmas matins are grander in another way."

By this time there were a great many other people on the road, both driving and walking, on their way to church. There was quite a procession of sledges, and such a jingling of bells as was delightful to hear, and the children had enough to do to listen and to ask questions.

They had by this time arrived at an open tract of country, and just before them, with its spire pointing towards heaven, and the dark green wood behind it, stood the church with lights streaming from every window, as if within were a sea of light. And at that very moment the church-bells began to ring.

The children were hushed into silence. They felt a solemnity come over them. They did not exactly know how they felt.

They soon dismounted. The church-bells rung, and light streamed out of the church, but all around it was dark and night-like. Along the whole extent of the church walls on every side, sledges were drawn up close together, the horses in which were eating hay. Among these a place was found for Polle; a covering was thrown over him, and between him and the church wall was laid a good bundle of the very best hay—real Christmas provender. Of this he ate; anybody might have heard how excellent he thought it.

The widow and the children walked across the church yard.

"Do you remember, children," said she to them, "what I told you about the Christmas matins, and what they mean?"

"They mean," stammered Erik, "they mean that—that God who—who"—"Who," interrupted the mother, "since the beginning of the world sent teachers and wise men to mankind, to—to,—now, Erik!"

"To teach them his will," said Erik.

"Yes, right," continued the mother; "and last of all, he came himself down to them, and condescended to be born on earth—"

"Yes, as a little child!" exclaimed Maja.

"Yes," answered the mother, "that he might pass through life with them as a brother, and might teach them rightly to understand his disposition, and how kind he meant by us all. And that is he whom we call the Son of God, our Saviour, Jesus Christ."

"And it is his birth which we celebrate in the Christmas matins," exclaimed Erik, now very certain of his subject.

With these words they entered the church, and all the congregation sang,

"Hail to the glorious morning hour!"

The children, however, could not think about singing. They could do nothing but stare about them and wonder. There was so much light! They could scarcely see for light. All the four grand chandeliers hung down from the roof blazing with lights. Upon the altar lights were burning in tall candlesticks. Upon the pulpit stood lights, and gilded branches extended from the walls, holding clusters of lights, and a light burned by every branch, so that the great aisle was like an alley of flame. Whichever way they looked, they saw light, light, light!

The benches were crammed full of people. Head was close to head. The children had never seen so many people together before, and they thought they should never find seats. At last, however, they did, on a bench where the people kindly made room for them. A respectable old woman took Maja on her knee, and the mother took Erik on hers. And thus they all were seated.

The children looked about incessantly, and stared at all the grandeur and splendour around them. But the mother soon forgot every outward object, for just then she opened her hymn-book, to join in singing the following verse of the hymn:

> "His tears, like ours, will fall as rain,
> A mourner, he will us sustain
>   With strength from heaven imparted;
> He will make known his Father's will,
> And mercy's holy balm instil
>   To soothe the broken-hearted."

With this the heavy leaden weight seemed to melt away from her soul, and her tears began to flow more easily.

She felt at once such a lightness and such a strength within her, that it seemed as if from this time nothing would be too heavy for her to bear.

The clergyman now ascended the pulpit, and what a sermon he preached! The widow had never heard any one speak in that way before. It seemed to her as if he spoke to her out of the warmth of her own innermost heart. And every single word seemed like a true word of God, so full of beauty and grandeur was it. To her it seemed as if the whole world, and the whole of life, became bright through it. It was as if it were Christmas matins within her soul.

And when she looked at Peter, she saw that he also listened attentively, with his eyes riveted upon the preacher; and from this, she hoped for a good result, more especially, as with the new year Peter was to begin to read with this same clergyman, preparatory to his confirmation.

When the service was ended, it was full daylight, and the congregation streamed hastily out. Before long, people might be seen on all sides, walking briskly along, driving on the road, or ascending the hill, striving who should first reach home; for, according to popular belief, they who arrive first at home on Christmas morning, will have their harvest first housed in the autumn Though what connexions there are between these things, I know not.

The widow and her children went into the poor-house, and the children themselves gave old Alle the meat and the bread which they had saved for him. For this they received the old man's blessing, and they felt, therefore, greatly pleased at what they had done.

In the mean time, Peter had been getting Polle and the sledge ready. Thus they drove home, thinking by the way of the delicious warm cabbage which they should have for dinner, for they all felt hungry and cold.

And how excellent were the meat and the cabbage which they had for dinner, it is not in my power to describe; this only is certain, that the king's cabbage could not have tasted better to him than theirs did to them.

In the afternoon they had also a cup of coffee, with cabbage, in honour of Christmas day, and that, too, tasted most excellently; and everybody was very cheerful, the widow as well as the rest; for she saw that the countenance of her elder son had undergone a change.

In the twilight, when they all sat together, warm and comfortable, and when the fire blazed merrily on the hearth, and lighted up the whole cottage, the mother said,

"Now, I wonder whether either of my little ones can remember anything of what the clergyman said in the morning about the Saviour, and what he taught to mankind?"

But, ah me! The poor little ones remembered nothing, not a word; had understood not a word—nay, had not even heard a syllable!

"There was such a deal of light!" they said.

"But you, Peter," said the mother, and looked at him with confidence, "I am certain that you can help me to recollect something of what the pastor said—you can remember it certainly."

"O, yes," said Peter, and his eyes brightened, and added he, after a moment, "I now know how people should live."

"Yes, and why?" said the mother looking kindly at her son, and wishing to try him.

"That they may follow after the Saviour, and labour for the world's redemption," said Peter, and raised his head; "and high and low, and rich and poor, can alike labour in this good work on earth."

"And how must that be done?" inquired the mother as before.

"By becoming better, more God-fearing, more righteous men."

"Yes, my son," exclaimed the mother, joyfully, "so did I also understand the words of the clergyman. By becoming so, by living in Christ, we help not only to extend God's kingdom on earth, but become also his labourers in the creation of a new heaven and a new earth, where bliss shall abide for ever. This is a great saying, my son, and can make the heart beat high and free even in a mean hut. And this have I known and believed from my youth upwards. But I have never heard it put rightly into words until to-day."

Peter was affected to tears; he extended his hand to his mother, and said with deep feeling, "Mother, forgive me that I have caused you sorrow! From this time it shall be otherwise!"

And from that time it did become otherwise with Peter; not that he ever became very communicative, or of a very cheerful temper, but he became very industrious, and very desirous of doing right, and everybody grew fond of him.

It was evident now that Peter began to take pleasure in life; at least, he never looked sour or sullen. His whole appearance was changed; nay, it often looked as if something shone within him, and so said his little brother and sister.

"Now it is Christmas matins with Peter," they would say.

Many Christmas matins have since kindled their lights; many a hard Christmas goblin has looked savage upon the Christmas board; has since then been shut up in a chest—thence brought out again to give strength to the beasts at plough. Yes, many a Christmas has, since that Christmas morning, come and gone; but the light that then was kindled for the mother, has never been extinguished.

Peter now lives as a peasant in Storgal, and his mother lives with him, and he likes to tell his friends what a sluggish and hard-tempered lad he was, and about the Christmas matins which produced such a change on him; and how, since then, he has had light, and strength, and pleasure in all his work, and how everything prospers in his hands.

Thus Peter celebrates every Christmas eve as his mother taught him. At Christmas matins he may be seen before any one else; and as for the Christmas goblin, he never forgets that!

MANAGING CHILDREN.

"My soul, look well around thee ere thou give thy timid infant onto sorrows."

One of the hot days of the last few weeks, it was my lot to be riding in the cars a long day's journey. When we started in the early morning the travelling was delightful. The country looked green and bright with the night's dew, and the soft, cool morning breeze refreshed us as it blew through the cars. But as we went on, the sun grew hotter and hotter, the dust blew into the cars mingled with cinders, and we all felt that for the rest of the way we were doomed to discomfort. I tried, with a book, to lose my sense of the present trials, but my attention was diverted from reading by a group which occupied the seat nearest me. It consisted of a mother, a father, and a little bright-looking boy of three or four years old. I noticed them when the cars first started sitting at a distance from me, but they had now changed their seats, and were so near to me that I could not avoid both seeing and hearing all that was going on.

"Be quiet, will you?" were the first words from the mother, said in an excited and impatient manner. But the little one could not be quiet. He had been travelling for many hours, he had exhausted all his means of amusement, and eaten cake and candy till he could eat no more. He had examined the cars over and over again, until the novelty was all at an end, and he was evidently hot and uncomfortable. As well might you tell the wind to stop blowing, as to tell him to be quiet. So he looked at his mother, and then began to tease and whine, and to say that he was tired and wanted some water. I thought she would sympathize with the little one, and try to amuse and comfort him. But the noise evidently irritated her. "If you are not still in a minute, George Henry, I'll throw you out of the window; I will do it." The child looked frightened for a minute, and seemed to think it would be a terrible fate. But his reason, and experience too, we may suppose, told him that this threat would never be carried into execution. He tried however for a little while to amuse himself with his mother's gloves, but they were snatched away from him, and then he was evidently compelled to begin again. "Mamma, mamma, I'm tired," and then came a louder demonstration. By this time the father had waked from his nap, in no very pleasant mood it seemed, for hearing the child's voice, he immediately made a dive at him, shook him, and boxed his ears violently. "There now, stop crying and be quiet." But that was evidently out of the question. He could not do it at once, and the mother joined her voice to say in the same impatient, angry way, "Hush, hush, I tell you, or you'll get it again!" As soon as possible the child stopped the loud voice, and cowed down in his seat with a sulky look, and a disturbed expression on his face. The next time I looked he had fallen asleep, much to my satisfaction, and his sleep lasted till we were near our journey's end.

Very much of this kind of treatment of children is

there in the world, and if there were not a kind Providence watching over these little ones to overrule the bad influences of early training, still smaller than it is would be the proportion of good men and women. How many parents there are who seem to forget the tremendous responsibility that rests upon them, the great work that God gave them to do when he put little children in their arms, and who act, instead, as if they sought only how to rear and educate them with the least trouble to themselves. They seem to begrudge the time it takes, as if their whole time were too much to give to the training of immortal souls. Oh, the impatience that seizes a little child and inflicts a punishment in the heat of an angry moment,—how much has it to answer for? Do not be surprised to see the temper of your child uncontrolled as he grows older. You have been teaching him day by day, from his infancy, by your own impatience, and hasty yielding to passion, when waywardness and carelessness have irritated you. Calmly, and quietly, and lovingly, must a child be governed. If severe punishment must be inflicted, if in no other way can obedience be gained, wait until every spark of angry feeling has left you, and let him see that you go about it solemnly and sadly.

This teaching children falsehood, too, by unmeaning threats; what a store of trouble is a parent laying up for himself who does it! Not in the smallest degree, not in the youngest child, ought it to be practised. The child will remember it; he will look back a few years hence; he will feel that it was false; and he may say, If falsehood is justifiable in one case it is in another; if in my mother, in me.

Love and tenderness go very far in the management of children; not a foolish indulgence that pampers the appetite and yields weakly to every foolish desire, but the quiet love that wraps the arms about the child, and lays cheek to cheek, and speaks so softly that the little one feels in his inmost heart that he is blessed by it; feels that he cannot slight it or disobey it. The rough boy on whom threats would be lost, who feels too proud to be afraid of punishment, will be melted, and be ready to give up darling plans, by such a love as this.

To educate children as God would have us, to feel a hope that we are fitting them for heaven, requires a life of watchfulness and prayer. Of watchfulness; lest we, by our example, by yielding to impatience or selfishness, may implant in the souls of our children, seeds that in coming years will bring forth bitter fruits. Of prayer; that we may be aided and strengthened by an Almighty hand.

THE MOTHER'S RESOLVE.

It was late tea-time at Mr. Merwyn's pleasant back parlour, in his commodious and comfortable house, in Boston. Mrs. Merwyn was sitting by the fire awaiting the return of her husband from his store. William and Anne, the children, were rudely racing round the room, overturning chairs and stools, and threatening every moment to upset the tea-table. "Stop, children, this moment," said Mrs. Merwyn. "Anne, open the door for your father; Willie, ring the bell for Bridget."

"Father has a night-key, and he can open the door for himself," said Anne; upon which she commenced a desperate struggle with Willie, to recover a toy he had snatched from her.

Mr. Merwyn entered the room with a jaded, tired look, and sat down by the fire. Soon after, Bridget came in with a plate of toast in one hand and a cream-pitcher in the other. The children, quite beside themselves in the eagerness of their quarrel, ran against her, knocked the dish of toast from her hand, and its contents were spread on the carpet. Mrs. Merwyn ran to them, and seizing them each in turn, boxed their ears soundly, accompanying her castigation with severe reproaches. "I never saw anything like it! You are the worst-behaved children I ever beheld! You are the plagues of my life! I wish you were, both of you, a hundred miles off! I am sure I cannot imagine how I came to have such bad children. Go to the table this minute, and see if you can behave yourselves. You make it very pleasant for your father, who has been working for you all day, to come home and find the house in such an uproar, and the carpet spoiled, and the toast gone." With such expressions, she drove the children to the table.

They were really pretty children, though pale and delicate; but now, with their unnaturally flushed faces, dishevelled hair, and angry looks, their appearance was anything but agreeable. They began to eat in moody silence. The parents were silent also. At length Mrs.

Merwyn said, "Willie, don't eat so much of that rich cake; take some bread and butter; and, Anne, stop helping yourself to sweetmeats; you have eaten two saucers full already."

"I don't like bread and butter," said William, in a surly tone, "and I can't eat what I don't like."

Anne, with a look of contempt at her mother, coolly helped herself to the last of the preserves, and ate them.

The evening passed as uncomfortably as it had begun. When the tea-things were cleared away, the study table was set out, for the children had lessons to recite on the morrow which must be learned in the evening. But they were cross and ill-natured to each other, and their father, after trying for half an hour to read a pamphlet which he had brought home with him, threw it aside, and seated himself with a heavy sigh by the fire.

"I say, mother," said Willie, "where's Turin?"

"I don't know exactly; look it out on the map."

"I can't, there's such a crowd of little names here; and, what's more, I won't. I don't care if I do miss in my lesson. I have got so low in my class now, I would as lief be at the foot as anywhere else."

"Mother, is *good* a noun or an adjective?" inquired Anne.

"How should I know?" replied the mother. "Can you not tell from the way in which it is used?"

"No, I can't," said Anne.

"Study your rules, then, and do not tease me about it," said the mother.

The books were put away. Nine o'clock came, and the children left the room for bed: Anne complaining of a headache, and upbraiding Willie for breaking her glass bird.

After sitting silent for half an hour, looking steadily into the fire, Mr. Merwyn turned round to his wife, who was seated near the table with her head upon her hand: the needlework had fallen upon the floor. "Helen," said he, "why do our children behave in the way they do? I want a cheerful, pleasant, orderly home. I have built this house, and furnished it handsomely, and I am sure I supply you liberally with every means of comfort, and yet how uncomfortable we are. And it all comes of those unruly children."

Mrs. Merwyn looked up half angrily. "If the children are bad, is it not partly your fault, James? Do you govern them as you ought?"

"How can I?" replied the husband. "Am I not at my work all day? And must I spend the time in which I need a little relaxation, in reducing a couple of rebellious children to order? They love me little enough now. It is seldom that I get the slightest caress, or even a respectful word from either of them; and how would it be if I spent my evenings in checking and scolding them? I took tea at our old friends, the Westons, last evening. Weston is as busy as I am, and the whole charge of their five children falls upon his wife; but, oh! Helen, it made my heart ache to see them; such happy cheerful faces, such intelligent looks, such pleasant, winning ways; so quiet and obedient, and yet so loving and affectionate to their parents and to each other! I used to hope my children would grow up so; but I have no such hope now—they grow worse as they grow older. I desire you will let them have another room to pass their evenings in, for I want to have them out of my sight." Having thus spoken, with a heavy sigh, the father left the room for his chamber.

When he was gone, Mrs. Merwyn burst into a passion of tears. The fountains of feeling seem stirred to their inmost depths. At first she pitied herself; she was angry with her husband and her children. She called to mind the fact that she was married at seventeen to a husband considerably older than herself. "And how could it be expected," thought she, "that I should know anything about bringing up children? I was a petted, indulged, half-educated girl, myself; where was I to get the strength, and the self-denial, and the perseverance necessary for this most difficult task? Was it to be expected that I should give up every pleasure of youth, and think and work entirely for others?" As these thoughts passed through her mind, she wept the more.

Mrs. Merwyn, it is true, was married too early; she had begun wrong. But she was a woman of deep feelings, and earnest, though unformed and undeveloped purposes. Having exhausted her self-commiseration, her thoughts took another turn. "But I love my children, and I love my husband. I am their mother. I am his wife; and do not nature and God and my own heart urge me to a higher and better discharge of duty than I have ever yet practised? Oh! how happy I should be if I could reclaim my children, reform them, and establish a mother's influence over them; if I could make my husband happy and his home delightful! What would I not sacrifice for this!" Her face beamed as she indulged in these bright visions, but reflection brought discouragement. "I am thirty years old," murmured she; "Anne is twelve and Willie ten. Even if I could change myself, how can I alter them? Ah! I fear it is a hopeless case."

Mrs. Merwyn had never made a profession of religion, though she had for some time entertained a kind of doubtful hope of her spiritual state, and had practised an earnest but irregular habit of secret prayer. She now sunk upon her knees, and laid all her sorrows, wishes, hopes, and half-formed resolutions, before the great Helper and Comforter; praying for wisdom and strength, as Solomon prayed when intrusted with the kingdom; for she felt, more deeply than ever before, that she, too, had a high and holy mission to fulfil, and that strength and guidance from above were absolutely necessary to enable her to perform her duty. She rose with a feeling new to herself: a calmness, a resolution, a determination, which inspired her with hope and confidence.

The next morning she went to her old friend, Mrs. Weston, and made her the confidant of her new feelings and plans. Mrs. Weston was a large-hearted, strong-minded, pious woman. She listened with generous interest, she encouraged, she advised: and, after a conference of three hours, Mrs. Merwyn returned home. That evening, after her husband and children had retired, she took her writing-desk and wrote the following schedule of resolutions:

"Resolved, That the first duty of the day performed by me shall be a prayer to Almighty God, and especially for strength and wisdom, properly to instruct, guide and govern my children.

"Resolved, That I will never permit either of my children, with impunity, wilfully to disobey me, or treat me with disrespect.

"Resolved, That I will earnestly strive never to act from an impulse of passion or resentment; but will endeavour to preserve my judgment cool, and my feelings calm, that I may clearly see, and truly perform my duty to my children.

"Resolved, That I will devote a certain portion of my leisure to daily self-instruction, in order to be able properly to instruct my children.

"Resolved, That I will watch over my own temper at all times, cultivate a habit of cheerfulness, and interest myself in the little matters of my children, that I may thereby gain their love.

"Resolved, That I will break off the habit of lounging; that I will give up the reading of novels, and that I will attend fewer large parties, and devote the time which I shall thus gain, especially to pursuits which will increase the comfort and happiness of my husband, and forward the best interests of my children.

"Resolved, That I will especially study the health of my children, reading on the subject, and asking advice of those who are more experienced than myself.

"Resolved, That I will not yield to discouragement from failure in my first attempts at reform; but will persevere, putting faith in the promises of God to all those who earnestly and faithfully endeavour to do their duty."

These resolutions looked very cold and formal to the

mother when she had done writing them. The writing was nothing; they were in her heart; but she folded the paper and locked it in her desk, as a memento, if she should ever feel herself falling into old habits of indolence and self-indulgence.

The next morning the family took their breakfast as usual, Anne and Willie coming in just as their father was about leaving the table. He was going to leave home this morning, to be absent four weeks; but there was no respectful salutation, no pleasant parting kiss, from these ill-behaved children, for the father who had spent his days in toiling for their welfare. "Bring me something handsome!" and "Bring me something nice!" they exclaimed, as they took their seats at the table.

"Where's my cup of coffee?" said Willie. "This white stuff isn't coffee."

"No," said his mother, "it is milk and water. I prefer that you should drink it for your breakfast."

"And I prefer the coffee," said Willie, in a very determined tone, "and I am determined to have it." And he stretched his hand toward the coffee-pot to help himself.

"Take the coffee away, Bridget," said Mrs. Merwyn. It disappeared.

"Where's my buttered toast and sausages?" said Anne.

"You will have neither this morning. There is good bread and butter, and you can have a mutton chop or a boiled egg, just which you prefer."

"I don't prefer either; I want sausages. If I can't have what I want, I won't eat anything."

"As you please," replied the mother, coolly.

The children looked at their mother and at each other. They did not know what to make of this resolute resistance to their wishes. They begged, teased and fretted; but it was of no use. They finally, with sullen looks, condescended to eat what was before them. "But I know one thing," said Willie, "if I can't have what I want for my dinner, I'll starve. And I have not washed myself all over for a week, and I don't intend to any more. And I shan't go to school this afternoon; father's gone, and I mean to stay at home and play; and won't you, Anne?"

Anne declared her readiness to join in this plan, and with this bravado they left the room.

The dinner was still more stormy and uncomfortable than the breakfast had been. The children went to school in the afternoon, but with red eyes and angry tempers. Nor was it much better at tea. They were moody and discontented, and as indulgence had hitherto been the mother's only means of management, she could not alter the state of things. A cheerful word or a kind smile was met with sullenness or indifference; it had no value.

After a wild, romping game, which the mother did not attempt to check, the study table was drawn out; but, before the books were taken, she placed her children in two chairs, and seated herself opposite to them. Her eye was moist and her voice trembled a little as she began to speak to them; but, as she proceeded, the strength of an earnest purpose soon dried the one and gave firmness to the other.

"My children," said she, "I love you dearly. I love

you, and your father loves you, because you are our children. We wish to make you good, that we may love you better. We wish you to be happy, which you cannot be unless you are good. God has given you to us, and has commanded us to train you up in the way in which you should go. He has commanded children to love and obey their parents. You are old enough to feel and understand how right this is. I was a very young mother, my dear children, when you were given to me. I was not twenty years old when the youngest of you was born. I was ignorant, indolent and careless. I am older now. I have seen the evils of carelessness and over-indulgence. I have observed, have read, and I have thought. I am now resolved to strive to train you in the right way, and as the first step and foundation, I am determined that you shall obey me. I do not think you love me or your father, as children generally love their parents; perhaps you never will; but you must obey us and treat us with respect."

The children had often seen their mother in a passion from their provoking ways, and had often felt the weight of her hand upon their ears; but they now felt that a new principle was at work. They were silent as she proceeded.

"I am not going to give you a long lecture, or to reproach you with the past. Our business is with the present and with the future. Many things, which you have till now indulged in, will, from this time, be entirely changed. I shall be changed. I shall not be the same mother I was a week ago; I hope I shall be a better one. Anne and William, I speak seriously to you; you are both old enough to understand me. If you fall into the right way at once, it will save trouble and make me very happy."

"Mother," said Willie, looking at her half in wonder, "I'm almost glad at what you've been saying. I love you better than you think for, and I am not half so bad as you suppose I am; but somehow the naughty feelings always seemed to come because you let them. I've told Anne fifty times that I wished you would *make* us mind."

Anne said nothing for some time, but seemed to be in deep thought. At last she said, "I've often wished that I could be like Alice Weston; but I don't know how I am ever going to learn to be good. I know I shall be cross and angry fifty times a day; I can't help it."

"There is One who can help us all, if we truly seek His help, my children. Let us ask it now."

They knelt, and the mother, with streaming eyes, prayed for that assistance which the great Father of all has kindly promised to those who sincerely seek his aid. The children were unusually thoughtful, and learned their lessons in silence. At bed-time, Mrs. Merwyn had usually asked her children for a kiss. Sometimes it was carelessly given, sometimes not; always considered rather as a favour from the children. This evening she did not ask them for a kiss, but kindly bade them good-night.

The very next morning, this awakened mother began upon her new plan. She rose early, and went to her children's room, to see that they were bathed and rubbed, and to teach them how best to do it for themselves; and she required them to be ready for breakfast punctually at the hour. She excluded from the table everything which she considered unwholesome. Some rich. high-seasoned dishes, which had been favourites, were banished for ever, and food plainer, yet excellent in its kind, was substituted. Mrs. Merwyn sent her children out to run and play half an hour before going to school, and the same on their return; and she fitted up a large spare room with every convenience for exercise when the weather should be stormy. She examined into her children's studies, and reduced their number. She procured the same books, and spent two hours a day in making herself thorough mistress of their contents, keeping constantly a little ahead of them in their lessons. She procured various books of reference, and learned, not only the text, but whatever she could find relating to it in compends, dictionaries, and encyclopedias; and it was surprising to see how the respect of her children increased, when they found that their mother knew, not only more than they did themselves, but, in many instances, more than their teachers.

All this was easy. It was a plain path, requiring nothing but ordinary judgment, and a little extraordinary energy. Not so with the moral self-culture and training of her children, which this mother had now in earnest undertaken. It was not so easy to supply proper motives to children who had always looked to some outward, sensual indulgence, as the reward, not only of mental exertion, but for being good. It was not easy for one who had lavished caresses indiscriminately, merely to gratify her own feelings, or to coax them to her purpose, to give a value in her children's eyes to a smile, a caress, a word of praise, to make them motives and rewards for good conduct. It was not easy to curb the stubborn and long-indulged will, to check the impatient temper, to change rude manners into respectful politeness. And yet it was wonderful to behold the progress, even here; so much is there in a resolute determination, in sustained and unflagging effort.

The early rising and the evening prayer had not been discontinued; and though the mother devoted so much more time than formerly to her children, she found she had more leisure for household occupation, general reading, and social enjoyment, than ever before. The energy called up for a particular purpose, extended itself into every department, and gave firmness and confidence to one who had hitherto been thought rather a weak woman. Her friends remarked a depth and earnestness about her, which they had never observed before; and she was gratified to perceive an increase of respect and consideration in all around her. These things, however, came later. Our business is with the first steps of this change; to show that it is possible to stem an erring course, to retrace a mistaken path in the outset of life. Notwithstanding the involuntary admission of Anne and Willie, that it would be better for them to be well-governed, they had, both from nature and habit, become too fond of having their own way, readily to give it up. During the first week of her trial, especially, if this young mother had not brought to her support every power of her nature, and every motive suggested by conscience, love, and hope,—if she had not been sustained by constant prayer and a daily increasing sense of duty,—she would many times have yielded, and the old state of things would have been established more firmly than ever. Many were the struggles with her children, but still more frequent were her self-wrestlings. To be firm without severity; to inflict a necessary pain when her heart was overflowing with love; to teach an impulsive disposition to examine, wait, and weigh; and finally, to require the penalty of strict justice; to inflict the exact degree of punishment which the case required; all this demanded painful effort. And still more painful was it to withhold the caresses which she had been in the habit of bestowing upon her children whenever they would condescend to receive them. Mrs. Merwyn had the good sense, in forming her new system of discipline, to strive to avoid a habit of petty fault-finding. Many trifles were passed without reproof, many disagreeable habits unnoticed, in the hope and belief that when the great principle of filial obedience was established, its healthy stimulus would naturally produce a better growth.

One evening the children had been impolite to each other while at supper. The mother took no notice. At the study table Anne had her slate and pencil, which Willie wanted. "I will have it," said Willie; "I want it for my sums. I am not going away up to my room for my slate and pencil, while yours is lying here doing nothing."

They both seized the slate and struggled. Anne, being the stronger, gained possession, whereupon Willie struck her. She struck back again. Their mother had observed it all.

"Children," said she, "put down the slate, and come to me."

Her voice was deep and sad, but calm and resolved. They did not dare to disobey. Each, however, according to custom, began to accuse the other in very strong terms.

"Be silent," said the mother. Her voice was lower and slower than usual, yet it was obeyed. "Anne, look me in the face, and tell me every circumstance of this quarrel; see that you tell it exactly." Anne felt that she must tell the exact truth, and she did so.

"Willie, now let me hear your account." Willie stated the facts exactly.

"My children," said the mother, "you are both to blame. You both deserve punishment; but I long for the time to come when we need not resort to punishment. Yesterday, for one fault, you forfeited a pleasant ride, which your uncle had offered to give you. Last evening, I was obliged to put you in separate rooms, and sit here alone by myself. This morning you each received five severe strokes upon the hand. It is painful for me to punish you; but this fault must be atoned for. Sit down at opposite sides of the table, and think. See if you cannot devise some way of getting along this time without punishment."

"Mother," said Willie, "I know what you mean; but it is the very worst punishment I could have. Must I ask sister's pardon?"

He looked at Anne, and she at him. He was naturally of a generous disposition, and there was something in his sister's countenance which touched a chord long unused to vibrate.

"Anne," he stammered out, "I *do* beg your pardon. Will you forgive me? I was most in the wrong."

"I did wrong, too," said Anne.

"Mother, will you forgive us?" said they both, with one impulse.

"I will," said she. "Now go to your lessons."

She was obliged to go to another room to conceal her emotion at this first conquest of her children over themselves; this first-fruits of her new system of training. "Help me, O, help me to persevere!"

And in the prayer with her children, before retiring to rest, she thanked Him for putting good, kind, and gentle thoughts into their young hearts; and prayed that this spirit might grow more and more, until Love should

"Through all their actions run."

That night, the children looked and lingered, before retiring to rest, as if in want of something; but no kiss, no caress, was offered by their mother, though her heart was yearning for it.

The next day was passed without the call for punishment. The evening was cheerful and happy. When Willie had looked ten minutes in vain to find a certain place in the south of Europe, on the map, his mother came and pointed it out to him, giving him at the same time some interesting particulars of its history and principal manufactures. "Thank you, mother," said Willie: "how much you do know!"

Anne had a piece of poetry to commit to memory, in which Circe and the Cyclops, and the Syrens were mentioned.

"How many thousand such make-believe beings our books are full of!" exclaimed she. "Where did the stuff all come from? Don't you think it all nonsense to study about them, mother?"

Mrs. Merwyn took the opportunity briefly to explain the ancient mythology. She gave a short account of Homer, repeating Byron's beautiful lines, and afterward a little sketch of Ulysses, as detailed in the Odyssey.

"How interesting!" said Anne. "How I should like to read the Odyssey! After all, though I don't believe a word of these old stories, it must be very pleasant to know all about them; for we are meeting with something or other about them in almost every book we see."

That evening, the children seemed more closely drawn to their mother than ever before. Her steady government, and her newly-discovered stores of information, had raised her wonderfully in the opinion of her children, and their love seemed to keep pace with their respect. And this evening her manner had been so kind, her voice so gentle; she had given up her own occupations to attend to them; she had refused a pleasant invitation in order to pass the evening with them. A good and gentle influence had seemed to settle upon them, tuning their minds to love and harmony. But bed-time came. The children looked wistfully at their mother. At last, Willie said, "Mother, you never kiss us, now. Won't you kiss us to-night?"

"Yes, my children. This has been a happy day to

me, because you both have been good children." Upon this, she kissed them fondly.

"Won't you always kiss us, when you think we have been good enough?" said Willie; "and then we shall know what you think about it."

"Yes, I will, Willie."

"Mother," said Anne, "when is father coming home?"

"In a week."

"I thought," said Anne, hesitating, "that fathers always governed the children. Father never governs us."

Mrs. Merwyn took that opportunity to explain to her children how dearly their father loved them, how constantly he exerted himself for their welfare, how worthy he was of their highest respect and love, and how much he would be gratified if they should strive in every way to improve themselves.

The week passed happily away. The children, finding they could gain no end by opposing their own will to the determination of their mother, ceased attempting it, while her judicious praise, whenever they really deserved it, gave them a pleasure so new and sweet as greatly to stimulate their efforts and increase their love.

On the expected evening, just at tea-time, the father came. The room was bright and clean. The fire was blazing. Extra lights burned on the mantel. A little feast was spread upon the table. The lessons had been learned beforehand, and the books put away. The mother had on a handsome new cap, and the children had asked permission to put on their holiday clothes. Mr Merwyn entered as he had left, with a pale and rather sad countenance. "My dear husband!" said the wife with a beaming face.

"My dear, dear father!" cried both the children, kissing him.

Willie drew his arm-chair to the fire. Anne took his overcoat and gloves, and carried them to the table. Then she smoothed his hair and brushed the dust from his coat, after which they both stood and waited till he should be warm and ready to go to the table. While at the table they were quiet and polite.

In the evening, the children amused themselves together with joining maps and puzzles, while Mr. Merwyn gave his wife the particulars of his journey. At bedtime, they came to their mother for a kiss, which she gave them. They then somewhat timidly approached their father. "Won't you kiss us, father?" said Anne: "mother says we have been good to-day." The father kissed them with glistening eyes.

When they were gone, he said to his wife, "Helen, now you are changed! How much brighter and happier you look than you did a month ago! and not only that, but you have grown suddenly taller, higher in mind and body. And the children—what has come over them? They are not the children I left; they are good, gentle, well-behaved. How is this?"

Then the wife, amid tears and smiles, poured into the ear of her listening husband the history of a month; her new-born resolutions, her trials, and now her beginnings of success.

"And have you accomplished so much in a month, Helen? It seems impossible."

"I have, to be sure, exerted every power of my nature. I resolved to make a change before your return, if it was in the power of human effort to do it. I trust I have made a beginning. I have discovered affections and capabilities in our children, which I never suspected. My dear husband, let us join together, let us persevere; and who knows but we may yet deserve and enjoy the blessing promised to faithful parents?"

"My Helen, I thought of little else during my long journey. I came home with my mind full of it. I had determined to alter many things in my business and domestic habits, entirely with reference to the best interests of my children, though, I confess, I was not sanguine in the hope of any thorough and radical improvement."

Hours passed, while the husband and wife communed of the future, making resolutions and forming plans to carry out, in the best manner, the reformation in their children, so happily begun.

It would be interesting to trace the steps by which these parents, now thoroughly awakened to a sense of duty, and the importance of the trust committed to their care, gained an influence over their children, which resulted in beautiful developments of character, and, finally, by the blessing of God, in a well-founded hope of happiness in a future life. It would be interesting to trace the progress of self-culture and self-improvement, by which they were enabled to do this; we can only record a brief conversation which took place about a year after the events we have been detailing occurred. Mrs. Weston, the good friend mentioned in the beginning of this story, had for several months been confined to the house by the protracted illness of one of her daughters. Her husband, coming in rather late, one evening, told her that he had been to take tea with the Merwyns.

"And how did you find them?" asked Mrs. Weston. "It is long since I have been able to see them."

"And I," rejoined Mr. Weston, "have kept away from them on purpose. They used to be always in trouble with their children. Their house was a very uncomfortable place."

"Is it better now?"

"Better! you would not know the children; you would scarcely know the parents. In the first place, the children have lost the pale, puny look they used to have; they were blooming with health and overflowing with spirits, yet they were not rude. I watched them. They were kind to each other, polite to me, and obedient to a word or a look from their parents. When I went in, they were studying their lessons, which they were anxious to finish before tea. When they were in difficulty they called upon their mother, and she gave them just that degree of help and encouragement which would make them think for and exert themselves. They had as good manners at the table as I ever saw in children. At eight o'clock, a company of young people came in, and I found it was a kind of regular Thursday evening soiree. Charades were acted, games were introduced; Merwyn and his wife occasionally joining, at the request of Annie or Willie, who seemed delighted when father and mother would take a part; mother, especially, was often called upon, and I could see the children's eyes sparkle with pleasure when she guessed right. The children evidently think there is nobody in the world like their mother.

"At ten o'clock, the young people went away. The children came for the good-night kiss, and I heard Willie whisper, as he put his arms round his mother's neck, 'Have I been good, dear mother? Do you love me?' I could not help asking about it. It seems that, about a year ago, they came to a determination to do their duty as parents. Helen says you helped her at the outset. Since that time Merwyn has never once omitted daily prayer. Never once have the children been permitted to disobey with impunity. The modes by which they have induced habits of veracity, of kindness, of self-denial, of politeness, of mental exertion, would be a pattern to most parents. Merwyn does not go to his counting-room after tea; he devotes himself to his family. And once a week, the children's holiday, they all go off to some country place, pic-nicking, flower-gathering, nutting, landscape-hunting, something to improve mind and body. Mrs. Merwyn has almost given up large parties; but she cultivates a circle of pleasant friends, and encourages social visits. Pray, go to see her, my dear, now Alice is better, and take the children."

"I will, my dear."

"Helen and you will agree exactly. Your notions are alike; but Merwyn is far, far ahead of me. My children love me, but they do not cling to me as Merwyn's do. I have cared for their outward and temporal welfare, but how little have I done for their higher and better interests! The burden has all been thrown upon you. I have not done my part. I am ashamed of myself. I am provoked—"

"Provoked to good works, I hope," said Mrs. Weston, with a kind smile. "That is the way friends should provoke each other. I am delighted with what you tell me, and I also will become a learner. It is never too late to improve. If parents generally would follow the example of these Merwyns, if they would with prayer and resolution *act* to reform their children, instead of repining and wrongfully accusing Providence, a blessing would fall upon their homes and their hearts. There would be light in their dwellings. Instead of the spirit of heaviness there would be joy and peace; and, at the last, they would hear the joyful words, 'Well done, good and faithful servant!'"

BE CAREFUL HOW YOU TREAT CHILDREN.

SISTER and I have been sitting to-night talking over our childhood's days. How many a word, act, and even look we remember, which the speakers or actors deemed we would forget with the passing hour! How we have been away in secret, and wept over lightly-uttered words, or even gentle reproof! Alas, some of them have carried their effects upon our whole after years! Children are quick to feel—quick to comprehend; much quicker than their elders usually deem. I remember now of the punishment a teacher inflicted upon me when quite a child. How unkind and unjust I thought her, then, and how void of the better feelings which I possessed! Before that I had loved her dearly; but I could never so love her again. The punishment came because I would not tell what had made me laugh outright during study hours. I would not tell, because it would have thrown the blame upon another. Child as I was, I well remember how my heart swelled within me to think I could bear and suffer for another; and even my teacher's insisting upon the wrong could not make me act it. She is dead, now; and can never know how long or how vividly I remembered her unjust punishment.

One can never be too watchful over himself in his dealings with children. Their perceptions are usually very quick, their hearts truthful and sincere. If they were ever and steadily thus dealt with by others, more would grow up truthful and earnest men and women. And, oh, how much we need such persons among us! It seems to me children are taught deception from their very cradles. No wonder they become such adepts in it in their after years.

Few parents have the patience to always do rightly and deal honestly with their children. And if *parents* have it not, how can it be expected that *servants* will? *They* work for hire; and many of them have no interest in their labours, save for the time being. Yet many mothers give up their children almost entirely to such care. They are young, and gay, and fashionable, perhaps, and cannot devote their precious time to the nursery. Society has claims upon them which must be answered. They strive to procure good servants, it may be, and then they have done their duty.

Oh, mothers, is this all your duty? When God gave those precious souls to your keeping, went there no "still, small voice" to your heart, saying, He would again claim them at your hands? Do not their eloquent pleadings—pleadings which every mother understands—woo you to a sense of the sweet, yet heavy responsibility resting upon you? Can you turn coldly away, and day after day, night after night, and week after week, leave them at Pleasure's or Fashion's fitful call? Could you do this, and yet hope for happiness here or hereafter? Ah! no, it cannot be! Nature's voice cannot be so silenced. It will speak out within the heart, if not to the world at large. I envy not the mother who is a devotee at Fashion's shrine. Rather give me laborious hours and weary vigils by the loved ones at home; so that, at last, I may "give up mine own with usury," feeling a certainty that I "have done what I could."

GRANDMOTHER'S STORY.

"All about,
The broad sweet sunshine lay without,
Filling the summer air."—LONGFELLOW.

It was a calm, shady summer afternoon. Such an afternoon as seems to me always a poem, rich, mellow, complete; with nothing of a turgid, stirring, *Ossian* swell about it; but a calm, soothing *Bryant*-poem, one of those afternoons that are Nature's "lullaby" to the soul.

I was at Valley Falls, at grandmother's. Somehow I am happier there than I am in the city, though my sisters would think it was very ungrateful of me, to say so when they buy me four new silk dresses every year, and I can ride down Broadway in their own carriage, every pleasant afternoon.

They are very fashionable ladies, my sisters. They live in great stone houses on Fifth Avenue, and when they sweep up and down their magnificent parlours, the blaze of their diamonds puts to shame the light of the chandeliers.

They are called very elegant and exclusive, my sisters, and dear me! what a strife there is among the ladies down town, to have their names on their visiting list—then their parties are said to be the most *recherché* of the season, and the dressmaker and milliner who can say they made Mrs. Devoe's last ball dress, or Mrs. St. Clair's beauty of a spring hat, think their fortunes are made. I am very unlike my sisters, and they say it is a source of constant anxiety to them. They tell me it betrays such a painful want of *musical* taste to prefer our old church organ to the opera, and the wind in the great maple branches at Valley Falls, to Jenny Lind's bird song.

Then too I love the green meadows, and the mountain daisies, and the cool sweet breath of the country clovers, and the broad, clear, sunshine, so much better than the drawing-rooms, with their dim, pink-rose light, their carved arches, and their Parisian carpets.

But as I was saying, I was at grandmother's, and my sisters were at Newport and Nahant; and I should have been with them, if mamma, before she died, had not exacted a promise that I should pass every summer at Valley Falls; and, so every June I say "good-bye" to the city, and with a heart glad as bees in May clover, or a bird among apple boughs, I come up here to the old gray "farm-house" where my mother lived, and where my grandmother once said, " would God she had died."

I was sitting by the window, where the plum boughs leaned up against the side of the house, and the green leaves brushed my forehead as they went to and fro to the low rhythm of the summer wind, when I heard the gate-latch unclose, and peeping between the branches, I saw a female coming up the walk. The sunshine fell full on her face and figure, so I could see her distinctly. She was an old lady; there was no relief to the thick white hair that was neatly parted, and gathered under her lace cap, for she wore no bonnet. There was a kind of solemn dignity in the old lady's manner, as she came up the walk, her black silk dress brushing the gravel stones.

There was an expression too in her face, that attracted while it repelled me. It was a proud face; time had gathered the once smooth forehead into thick wrinkles, and hollowed the cheeks, and sharpened the mouth, but no work of time could erase the expression of those features. Even in death you felt it would be still *a proud face.*

But it was a mournful one; not the mournfulness alone of old age, and a heart weary, and almost done with life, but that of a mighty grief, an ever-present, ever-living sorrow.

There was a strange expression too in the eyes. I did not observe this at first; not until she passed in front of the house, and they wandered eagerly all over it, as though she were searching for some person at all the windows.

There was an indescribable somewhat in those eyes that terrified me, as at last they alighted on my face.

The old lady drew under the tree. "Good afternoon, miss," she said with a stately dignity that was strangely impressive.

"Have you seen Maurise this afternoon?"

"No, madam, I have not," I answered, divining at once that my questioner was labouring under mental aberration, "I am not acquainted with the person of whom you speak."

"Mrs. Hillyard!" called out a voice before the old lady had time to reply, and then I saw a plainly dressed, middle-aged woman, hastily coming towards her.

"My dear madam," she said, "we have been searching for you everywhere. How could you walk so far without either bonnet or shawl, in this warm sun? I have brought yours with me, and we had better return now."

"But I thought Maurise might have passed this way," said the old lady doubtingly, as she received the bonnet.

"No, I am quite certain she has not;" answered her companion in a soothing tone. "Nobody has seen her."

The old lady sighed so mournfully, that it brought the tears into my eyes. She took the arm of her attendant, between whom and myself a quick signal of intelligence had passed, and they went out.

Of course my curiosity was greatly excited. "Grandma knows everybody in these parts;" I murmured to myself, "and as soon as her afternoon nap is over, I'll go down and ask her who in the world Mrs. Hillyard is."

"Grandma, oh! I am so glad to find you are up, for the oddest circumstance happened about half an hour ago;" and I related the singular occurrence to which I had been a witness.

"Poor Mrs. Hillyard!" said my grandmother, shaking her head and sighing, "how true it is that God contemneth the 'high look, and the proud heart.'"

"Tell me all about it; won't you, grandma? I am just in the mood for hearing a story now, and I know this will be so interesting;" and I drew a stool to my grandmother's feet, as I always do to anybody's, if I dare, when they tell me a story.

It was just the time and place for telling one. I want you to mind this, and to *feel* that you are there too, while I relate it in my grandmother's own words.

It was a bedroom at the corner of the house, the cosiest, most comfortable little nook in creation. A thick vine grew over the low window and filled the room with a cool fresh dimness, like that of wood shadows, and the wind came up to us with a low pleasant rustle, which always fills the heart with sweet thoughts. Oh! there is no place for telling stories like a bedroom in the country.

My grandma gave two or three preliminary motions to her rocking-chair, and commenced.

"You remember, Luella, the large old house we passed yesterday, when we rode down to the Falls?"

'What," I said, "the one with the gray front, and the brier clambering over the steps, and such a mournful, *grave*-yard atmosphere about it, that I couldn't help shuddering as we passed it?"

"Yes, but once, Luella," and grandma's hand was laid fondly on my head, "a being, young and fair, and light-hearted as you are, sprang gracefully down those old stone steps, and her sweet laugh woke up the echoes that have long slumbered round the old house.

Mrs. Hillyard was a proud woman, and her pride has been her ruin, and, alas! not hers alone.

Her husband was a young man, when he brought his fair but haughty-looking bride to Valley Falls.

He was a kind, genial-hearted man, too, and the neighbours often wondered what induced him to wed a woman so cold and inaccessible as Mrs. Hillyard proved herself in all her intercourse with the people.

They said she came from an old but decayed English family, and it may be that education had developed and matured this inherent pride. I cannot tell; but it is best to deal gently as we can with those whom God has smitten.

Mrs. Hillyard loved her husband. I had no doubt of that, from the hour that I first saw them together; for a sudden light would kindle up the cold proud face whenever he addressed her, and sometimes, I have heard the soft tones grow eager, and full of womanly affection as they answered him.

We were never intimate, Mrs. Hillyard and I, still we always interchanged formal visits; so my opinion of her character was founded rather on personal observation, than on the remarks which her coldness and exclusiveness induced from envious and gossiping neighbours.

Years rolled on, Mr. Hillyard was slowly amassing a fortune in his profession, and one fair child had opened a new fountain of love in the heart of his wife, when one day, on returning from some neighbouring village, his horse took fright.

Mr. Hillyard, if I remember right, had purchased him only the day before, and probably did not understand managing the terrified animal.

At all events, after dashing over the main road for some two miles, he threw his rider; Mr. Hillyard was discovered and carried home to a bed from which he never arose. He lived only two days.

I remember how my heart ached for the almost distracted wife. I always believed it was nothing but the little Maurise who saved her mother from following her father.

The grief of the poor woman was terrible to behold. They were obliged at last to carry her by force from the body of her dead husband; and yet, I have sometimes looked out on the marble urn that rises among the thick hemlock trees, and thought it would have been better if *two* hearts were lying beneath it.

But Mrs. Hillyard lived, and Maurise grew into womanhood. I can see her now, (and my grandmother dropped her voice as though she were talking quite to herself.)

She had the pure, oval features of her mother, with the dark eyes, and bright smile of her father. Her hair was that golden colour that seems always fading off into a rich bronze shade, and her eyes always reminded me of the violets that grew when I was a girl deep in the shadows of the mountains."

"And was she as good as she was beautiful, grandma?" I whispered.

The old lady started as though she had quite lost sight of her hearer. " Yes, Luella, Maurise's nature was as pure, and gentle, and vine-like, as her mother's was cold, stern, and self-reliant.

Mrs. Hillyard loved her child with all the strength of her proud, exclusive nature, and so Maurise's feet came up through green paths to her early womanhood.

Then, for the first time at a fair in the old church, Austin Enfield met Maurise Hillyard. He was a young physician, who had received his diploma the previous winter. He was poor, his mother was a widow residing in an adjoining village, and it was reported that she had bound shoes, and so defrayed a portion of her son's expenses through college. But, physically and intellectually, Dr. Enfield was a noble specimen of young manhood, and I do not wonder when the deep, rich tones of his voice first greeted the ear of Maurise Hillyard, that her graceful head was turned quickly, and her blue eyes looked eagerly in his face.

They were mutually fascinated. The young doctor possessed peculiar conversational talent, and in our quiet, out-of-the-way village, Maurise had never met his equal.

Well, they went home to dream of each other, I suppose, and the next day, as Maurise was walking out, the doctor met her, and judging by the length of their absence they must have achieved quite a pedestrian feat that afternoon.

The doctor had engaged to pass that summer at Valley Falls; hence he and Maurise were thrown constantly together.

Mrs. Hillyard was an indulgent mother. She was proud of the attentions her daughter received, as the doctor was quite the lion of Valley Falls, and very injudiciously (considering her ambitious projects for her daughter's future) allowed the doctor's visits.

You have guessed the rest, Luella, I see it in your eyes.

One night, in early September, the doctor, as was his custom, accompanied Maurise home from singing school. They paused in the old grove of pines, where you say the wind is always singing mournful love ballads. There the young doctor told the story of his love.

Maurise's shadow-filled eyes were very bright with tenderness, as she answered, "If mamma consents, I will be your wife, Austin."

They went home; the doctor left her at her mother's gate; Maurise went in, laid her bright head in her mother's lap, and told her what she had said.

"Maurise, my daughter," and for the first time those calm, low tones sent a chill to the girl's heart. "You shall never be the wife of Austin Enfield."

"But, mother, I love him so, it will break my heart to give him up. I cannot, I cannot!" Maurise's voice crushed down her sobs as she repeated it.

The night was coming up into the gray shadows of

morning. before the mother and daughter separated. It had been a season of extreme suffering to both.

Maurise had proved that she inherited some of the character and firmness of her parent.

All the mother could urge in defence of her adverse position was the poverty of the doctor, and his family's want of social eminence.

"I never *can*, I never will give my consent, Maurise," she repeated. "You, whom I yet hope to see the wife of one of the first men in our country—*you*, wedded to a beggar!"

"*A beggar!* mamma." The sweet face flushed with anger. "For the sake of your child, do not couple that name with Austin Enfield."

"Well, he is neither rich nor honourable among men. If he were, you should have my consent to your union. As it is, I shall never grant it."

"Don't, mother, unless you would kill me, say this! Only tell me, if he wins riches and distinction, I may be his wife. We are both young, and can wait many years, and patiently."

And the mother looked on the pleading, tear-stained face of her child, and the woman that was in her relented.

"If he earn wealth, and can place you in a social position which will do you honour to be his wife, then, and only then, Maurise, will I consent."

The next day the doctor called. Mrs. Hillyard had a long interview with him.

It was decided that Maurise should wait five years,

and that during that time no intercourse, except what passed under the mother's supervision, should occur between them.

The doctor was to leave Valley Falls immediately. If he was successful in his profession during that period; if he could place Maurise in an elevated social position, at the end of that time, Mrs. Hillyard would no longer oppose their union.

"You have heard my stipulations. You can accede to them or not. I have only presented them because this thing involves the happiness of my child," was the not very flattering conclusion of Mrs. Hillyard's remarks that morning.

But the doctor was young, and his nature was high and hopeful. Moreover, he loved Maurise as he could never again love woman; so he said to her stately mother,

"I will accede to your propositions, Mrs. Hillyard, hard as they seem to me. In five years, if God prospers me, I will come back, and claim your daughter."

The young couple had a brief interview that morning, and then they separated for five years.

Time wore on. Dr. Enfield went to Europe to seek that fortune which alone would entitle him to the hand of Maurise; for, in her last interview with him, the girl had said,

"Austin, I will never wed any other man; but, even as your wife, I could not be happy with the curse of my mother on our union."

Two years went by. Austin wrote very hopefully to his beloved, and she had begun to dream of the time when her bright head should lie again in the sheltering of his arms.

It was in the soft June days that a gentleman, who was travelling through the interior of the state, stopped one Saturday afternoon at Valley Falls, and, as it was late, concluded to wait till Monday before prosecuting farther his journey.

On the Sabbath he attended morning service, and there he saw Maurise Hillyard. I remember how she looked that morning as though I had seen her yesterday. Her new blue hat harmonized so completely with her pure complexion, and its drooping lilies of the valley trembled against her flushed cheeks as she came, graceful and reed-like, up the old church aisle, behind her mother.

The rustle of her lilac silk, the waving of her embroidered cape, yet live in my memory; and the small fingers clasped over her hymn book come back, to complete the sweet vision of early womanhood.

Mr. Wilmot, the stranger, was a middle-aged and noble-looking man, with that indefinable air, made up of courtliness and character, which at once distinguishes the accomplished gentleman.

He had borne, with undisturbed equanimity, the curious glances of the five hundred eyes that greeted his entrance into the old church; but when Maurise passed before him, a sudden start and a visible change came over the gentleman's face.

She sat where he could have a distinct view of her face during the service; and, it must be admitted, his eyes wandered oftener to the maiden than to the minister that morning—and I doubt not but her mother, though she sat calm and erect as usual, was quite aware of this fact.

Mr. Wilmot did not leave Valley Falls the next day, as he stated to his host he should do.

It was very easy for him to procure an introduction to Mrs. Hillyard and her daughter, which he did, through the intervention of the squire, that same evening.

Mrs. Hillyard learned, through this latter gentleman, that Mr. Wilmot was a widower and a millionaire; and from that hour the ambitious mother formed a project, which her bright child, who was to be its victim, little dreamed of.

No efforts, within the mother's limited means, had been spared to render Maurise's education equal to the position which her parent had dreamed always she should occupy, and Mr. Wilmot found the country girl as intelligent as she was beautiful.

He was exceedingly agreeable in manner and conversation, and he was so much older than Maurise, and his attentions were bestowed in such a quiet, half-fatherly manner, that the girl little suspected what an intimate relation they had with her future.

So she laughed and sang, she walked and rode with Mr. Wilmot, and her mother looked on, with her sweet, cold smile, and planned and exulted.

At the end of two weeks, business imperatively summoned Mr. Wilmot from Valley Falls. The night before he left he had a long interview with Mrs. Hillyard; and the offer he made her child was certainly a flattering one, though he had three children, and was as old as Maurise's father.

"I will give your child an old name and an honourable one; I will surround her loveliness with every luxury that pride and my great wealth can procure; and in the home to which I shall take her, her beauty and her intelligence will win her the homage they deserve."

And the mother laid up his words in her heart, and in an evil hour they brought forth ruin, despair, and *death*.

"Maurise, my child, come, and sit down at my feet."

The mother's voice was very tender that evening, and Maurise went to her feet, and laid her little hands in her lap.

And then her mother told the astonished girl the proud offer that Mr. Wilmot had made her. Oh! it was a gorgeous future the ambitious woman painted for her child! A future to dazzle the brain, and lead astray the heart of a girl of twenty; and thus she concluded, kissing the uplifted forehead:—

"And now, dear, Mr. Wilmot said he would return in a month for my answer; and then shall I not tell him my Maurise will be his bride?"

Those blue, bewildered eyes moved not from the lady's face while she spoke; but Maurise answered,

"Mother, have you forgotten my troth-plight to Austin Enfield? I can never marry another man."

"Nonsense, my child; it is quite time you had lost sight of that foolish dream of your girlhood. Your life will be far above the plodding way on which Austin Enfield would take you. Come, it is high time you should forget him!"

"Never, never, mother, till I lie down where my heart will put aside its memories for ever, will it forget Austin Enfield!"

She syllabled the name with a world of tenderness, as she sprang from her mother's feet, her eyes brightening like night-stars off which rolls suddenly a summer cloud.

I know not whether it is true, but the neighbours say that the light in Mrs. Hillyard's drawing-room burned again till the gray of the morning, as the mother and the daughter sat there; and they say more than this, that at last the proud woman knelt at the feet of her daughter, and implored her, in the name of her mother's love, to become the wife of Mr. Wilmot.

And Maurise answered through her sobs, as she covered her pale face, to shut out the vision of her kneeling mother,

"I cannot, mother, for I do not love him!"

I do not know, Luella, at what time the tempter came to the heart of Mrs. Hillyard, and first whispered that dark deed, for whose perpetration she paid so dearly. I know not what struggle the quiet of her own chamber, or the stars of midnight witnessed. I only know that the evil conquered.

―

"Maurise, I have had a letter to-day. Can you guess from whom?"

Maurise could not see her mother's face as she said the words, for the lady was bending over her sewing.

"No. I'll give it up at once, mamma." The girl looked up from her book, and answered indifferently.

"It was from Austin Enfield, and I thought *you* might be interested in its contents."

The book dropped from Maurise's fingers. Her face grew pale, and her eyes bright.

"What did he say, mamma?"

"Something which you should know, my child; and yet I am reluctant to tell you, for fear it will give you pain."

"No matter. Tell me quick, mamma; anything is better than suspense." Her voice was quick and husky.

And Mrs. Hillyard told her daughter that the doctor had written from Italy, requesting that their engagement might be annulled—doubting not, as he said, that the matured judgment of Miss Hillyard would concur with his own in this matter, as it probably originated on her part, as it did on his, in a childish partiality, of which late years, more especially *late attachments*, had taught him the weakness.

Maurise rose up, and went to her mother's side. She was very calm, but the shroud-plaits were never drawn over a whiter face.

"Mother," she said, "let me see that letter!"

Her mother took it from her pocket, and laid it in her hands.

And Maurise read it; his own words in his own handwriting. She gave it back quietly, as she had received it.

"Come, darling, don't look so, for it troubles me.

He was not worthy of you, and I would forget him at once. Shall I write that you will release him?"

Maurise put her hand to her forehead.

"Yes; tell him this without delay. At least I will not stand in the way of his happiness."

Her eyes had a strange, far-off look in them as she said the words; and she turned to leave the room, and with her second step sank senseless to the floor.

"And he did not write that letter, the doctor did not write it," I whispered, drawing closer to my grandmother.

"No, dear. She wrote it herself, the day before, with his last letter to her child lying before her—that letter full of the great love and the high hopes that were in his heart.

I must hurry through with the remainder of my sad history, Luella, for the sun is sloping westward.

In a month Mr. Wilmot, as he had stipulated, returned, and Mrs. Hillyard met him in the parlour, and whispered,

"My daughter has consented. She will be your wife."

In two weeks they were married. There was a wedding festival such as Valley Falls had never witnessed. There were crowds of city guests, and the beauty of Mr. Wilmot's village bride was the theme of all their lips. They were married in the morning, and bridal crown never rested on brighter head, and bridal vows were never breathed by sweeter lips; and yet, as the sun came from behind a cloud, and fell like a sudden glory all about her, I had a full view of her face, and there was something in it that made my heart ache for her.

—

Two years had passed. The spring was late that season, and in the early June the tree branches were swinging in the wind, heavy with the beautiful blossoms of May.

Mrs. Wilmot has come home to pass a week with her mother. Her life in New York had been a scene of dazzling triumph. Her beauty and her elegance had won for her all the admiration her husband had predicted. I do not know whether she was happy. I only know that her manners had a calm, stately repose, very unlike the ardent, impulsive, light-hearted girl we remember at Valley Falls. But that summer she seemed more like her old self than ever. She went down in the meadows, and off in the springing wheat fields, and again the old echoes woke up to the light rich laugh of her girlhood.

Late one afternoon, Mrs. Wilmot and her mother sat together in the old sitting-room. The former had been relating, to her proud, attentive listener, a history of some of the most brilliant parties she had attended the preceding season, the dinners she had given, the toasts that had been drunken in her honour, and matters of like character, when she broke off, suddenly :—

"How exquisitely beautiful those apple-blossoms are! Do you remember, mamma, how I used to twine them in my curls every May-time? I used to say they were prettier than diamonds; and now I have tried these,

I'll see if my old taste doesn't hold good yet;" and, springing from her chair, she went out into the garden.

The little hands at last succeeded in reaching the lowest branch, and Mrs. Wilmot was breaking off a sprig of the white blossoms, when the stage rolled suddenly up to the front gate, and a young gentleman alighted a few yards from her.

He looked eagerly over the grounds and building until he espied Maurise; then he advanced quickly towards her. He stretched out his arms, and cried, in a voice trembling with glad tenderness,

"Maurise, Maurise, I have come back to you!"

The lady grew white as the blossoms that dropped around her. For a moment her light figure wavered to and fro like the apple-branches; but as the young man attempted to seize her hand, she drew it hastily away, and stood very still as she sternly, scornfully confronted him.

"How dare you address me thus, Austin Enfield, when you yourself first forfeited the right to do it; when I am now the wife of another?"

He sprang from her as though suddenly electrified. His face was whiter even than hers, and for a moment it worked fearfully as he stared at her, apparently not comprehending what she had spoken.

"Maurise, I do not understand you."

"Yes, you do. You remember the letter you wrote, requesting our engagement might be broken; and why have you come now, when I was growing happy again, to disturb my wedded peace?"

She hardly knew, in her excitement, what she was saying, but she was turning from him.

"Maurise! Maurise!" He sprang into her path, and held her back. "Hear me! You *shall* hear me! I never wrote such a letter; I never dreamed of such an act. God is my witness, I never did it!"

They went back together, and talked for an hour, under the still shadows of the great apple-tree. What they said there, God only knows; but when Doctor Enfield went out from it, he looked ten years older.

Maurise rose up. The sun had gone over the hill. She went slowly towards the house, still holding the crushed apple-blossoms in her hands.

Her mother came to the door to meet her; but she started, and drew back, when she looked in her face.

Her child drew up to her, and whispered in her ear,

"Mother, Doctor Enfield has just come out from the garden gate. We have learned all. You have betrayed your child, and broken her heart!" And she went up stairs, to her own room, and her mother could not answer her.

The next day there was a report through Valley Falls that Mrs. Wilmot had been suddenly seized with brain-fever, and that Mrs. Hillyard herself was hardly able to leave her apartment.

The best physicians and the most skilful nurses were procured. But each night the reports were less favourable—the younger lady was no better, but rather grew worse.

I was acquainted with the nurse who attended Maurise during her illness. She was truly a judicious, faithful woman; but she has since confidently told me it was the saddest sick-bed she ever watched over. Her moans for Austin Enfield; her shrieking entreaties to her mother; her wild prayers for help, were sounds which would haunt her memory till all sound would to her be *silence*.

One night (I must hasten over this, Luella, for I cannot dwell on it) Mrs. Wilmot seemed quieter than she had been for several previous days, and the nurse, whom constant watching had completely exhausted, left the sick lady in charge of a woman who had been hired the previous day, to occasionally relieve her in her arduous duties.

It was two o'clock when the nurse rose and went into Mrs. Wilmot's room. The night-lamp was burning dimly on the table, and the watcher sat by it in a heavy slumber; but the *bed was empty! the sick woman was gone!*

The house was alarmed; the neighbourhood was aroused, and that night Valley Falls was vainly searched for the sick woman. I cannot describe the agonies of the frantic mother, to which remorse must have added a tenfold bitterness, although no one at the time dreamed of this. She had seen her daughter but twice during her illness, having been carried thither both times, as she was too feeble to walk.

Dr. Enfield was riding down to Valley Falls, from a neighbouring village, the next morning. He had heard of Maurise's illness, and he knew, as none but her mother did, the circumstances which had occasioned it. He could not leave the vicinity while she remained in this state, and accordingly came down each day to learn the reports of her health.

His road lay near the bank of the river. The current is, as you know, a very strong one, and as the doctor looked off on the blue waters rolling out in the morning sunshine, something white arrested his attention. He was half convinced it must be the body of a woman, as he strained his eyes to distinguish the object, for he could see the long yellow hair floating on the waves.

Something in that bright hair sent a chill to the doctor's heart. He tried to alight, but he sank back in his carriage, and a strange faintness came over the strong man.

Some men were working in a meadow, a few rods distant. The doctor made a sign to them, and they came to his carriage. He pointed to the object in the river.

Two of the men sprang in immediately, succeeded in reaching the body, and bore it ashore. Then the doctor looked down on the cold, dead face, round which lay the wet, bright hair, and he saw——"

"Oh, grandma, don't say it was Maurise; don't, don't!" I cried, shuddering through my sobs, as I laid my arms about her waist.

My grandmother answered only by her tears, and they fell thick as raindrops on my bowed head.

"They carried her home, (she continued at last.) Her mother saw them coming up the walk, and, weak as she was, rushed out, and met them on the steps. One long, wild, eager look she gave to that dead face. Then the truth broke upon her. She thrust her arms upward, with a laugh that curdled the blood in the very veins of those that heard it, and from that hour to this she has been—what you have seen her, Luella."

"And her husband and the doctor—what became of them, grandma?"

"A messenger was despatched for the former, and the broken-hearted husband came, and saw all that was left of his beautiful, his idolized Maurise. He had not been apprised of her illness, as Mrs. Hillyard had forbidden this, fearing, I suppose, that in her delirious ravings her daughter might reveal more than it was well he should know.

But the doctor attended her funeral. She was buried by her father; and before the two gentlemen left they had a long interview. It is supposed that all was revealed at that time to Mr. Wilmot. Both gentlemen probably felt that God's retribution was fearful, and greatly as she had sinned, they must have pitied the wretched mother.

The doctor returned to Europe. I have never heard from him since. Mr. Wilmot married again some three years after the death of his wife.

It is generally believed that Maurise left the house that night, and threw herself into the river, in a state of high delirium, produced by brain-fever; but the *cause* of that fever is known by few."

"There, Luella, goes the supper-bell! Come, my child," and my grandmother lifted my face, and kissed it tenderly.

The sun had gone down, and the twilight was build

ing up its shadows in the corners of the bedroom. The wind had taken up a new hymn, the soft doxology of the day. The quiet and the beauty filled my heart with a prayer:—

"May God keep me from the sin of pride!"

"Amen!" said my grandmother, as we rose up, and went out.

I DREAMED OF MY MOTHER.

I DREAMED of my mother, and sweet to my soul
Was the brief-given spell of that vision's control:
I thought she stood by me, all cheerful and mild
As when to her bosom I clung as a child.

Her features were bright with the smiles that she wore,
When heeding my idle-tongued prattle of yore;
And her voice had that kindly and silvery strain
That from childhood had dwelt in the depths of my brain.

She spoke of the days of her girlhood and youth—
Of life and its cares, and of hope and its truth;
And she seemed as an angel just winged from above,
To bring me a message of duty and love.

She told of her thoughts at the old village school—
Of her walks with her playmates when loosed from its rule—
Of her rambles for berries, and when they were o'er
Of the mirth-making groups at the white cottage door.

She painted the garden, so sweet to the view,
Where the wren made its nest and the pet-flowers grew—
Of the trees that she loved for their scent and their shade,
Where the robin, and wild-bee, and humming-bird played.

And she spoke of the greenwood which bordered the farm,
Where her glad moments glided unmixed with alarm—
Of the well by the wicket, whose waters were free,
And the lake with its white margin traversed in glee.

And she pondered delighted the joys to retrace
Of the family scenes of that ruralized place,—
Of its parties and bridals, its loves and its spells—
Its heart-clinging ties, and its saddened farewells.

She pictured the meeting-house, where, with the throng,
She heard the good pastor, and sang the sweet song—
Of the call from the pulpit,—the feast at the shrine,
And the hallowed communings with feelings divine.

"And listen, my son!" she did smilingly say,
"If 'tis pleasant to sing it is sweeter to pray—
If the future is bright in the day of thy prime,
That brightness may grow with the fading of time.

"As the bow bringeth promise while arching the skies,
With its beautiful glory emblazed on the eyes—
Though blended with ether its loveliness fade,
The splendour is lost not, but only delayed.

"What healing like hope's shall the mourners restore,
When their sad bosoms sigh over pleasures no more,
As back to the place of departure they gaze,
Where the moonlight of memory mellowly plays?

"But thy present, my son, as its brief moments flee,
Is the prize to be seized and be cherished by thee—
'Tis the earnest of joys that no time can impair,
And is linked with a peace that I may not declare.

"And when the frail strength of humanity fades,
And darkness the eye-ball of nature invades,
From thy Pisgah of Hope 'twill be sweet to behold
What a Canaan of glories her hand has unrolled.

I DREAMED OF MY MOTHER.

"Look up to thy Maker, my son, and rejoice!"
Was the last gentle whisper that came from that voice,
While its soft soothing tones on my dreaming ear fell,
As she glided away with a smiling farewell.

There are dreams of the heavens, and dreams of the earth,
And dreams of disease that to phantoms give birth,
But the bearer of angels, awake or asleep,
Has a vision to love, to remember and keep.

I woke from the spell of that visit of night,
And inly communed with a quiet delight,
And the past, and the present, and future surveyed,
In the darkness presented, by fancy arrayed.

I thought of the scenes when that mother was nigh,
In a soft sunny land and beneath a mild sky,
When at matins we walked to the health-giving spring,
With the dew on the grass, and the birds on the wing.

Of the draughts at the fount as the white sun arose,
And the views from the bluffs where the broad river flows—
Of the sound from the shore of the fisherman's strain,
And the sight of the ship as it sailed to the main.

Of the wild-flowers plucked from the glen and the field,
And the beauties the meadows and gardens revealed—
Of all that she paused to explain or explore,
'Till I learned in my wonder to think and adore.

And of joys that attended the fireside scene,
When woodlands and meadows no longer were green—
Of the sports, and the tales, and the holiday glee,
That ever were rife at that fond mother's knee.

Of the duties of home, and the studies of school,
With the many delights that divided their rule,
'Till the sunshine of boyhood had ended, and brought
The cares and the shadows of manhood and thought.

And I sighed for the scenes that had faded away—
For the forms that had fallen from age to decay—
For the friends who had vanished, while looking before
To paths that their feet were forbid to explore.

And glancing beyond, through the vista of time,
With a soul full of hope, and with life in its prime,
Though flowers by memory cherished had died,
Life's garden was still with some blossoms supplied.

And oft as that dream to my spirit comes back,
A newness of thought re-illumes my track;
For it seems as a spell undefined and alone,
Of something concerned with the vast and unknown.

MOTHERS, DO YOU SYMPATHIZE WITH YOUR CHILDREN?

ROBERT MOLTON was very fond of his aunt Mary. Nothing ever gave him greater pleasure than the permission to spend a few days with her—he loved so dearly to listen to her stories. Indeed, it was a pleasure to sit down at any time and have a talk with Aunt Mary, if she did not tell a single story. Robert could bear to hear her talk, even about his faults, far better than he could bear it from any other person. But, for some reason, Robert was a better boy and exhibited fewer faults when with Aunt Mary, than at any other time.

"I wish," said Robert to his aunt Mary, one day, "that mother would talk to me as you do. If she would, I believe I should be a better boy when I am at home."

"I do not understand you, Robert," replied his aunt; "I am sure you have one of the kindest of mothers, who loves you as well as a boy can ask to be loved."

"I know my mother loves me," Robert replied. "She would *do* anything in the world for me, I really believe: but when I do anything she does not like, she don't talk to me as you do, but she—"

Here an awkward pause ensued. Aunt Mary waited for Robert to finish his sentence, but it was left unfinished after all. Robert was going to say, "she does scold so, it makes me so angry," but he well knew that his aunt Mary would not approve of his talking in that way about his mother. He tried to think of some other word which would express the same thing, and be less exceptionable, but of all the words in the English language which occurred to him, no other word but "scold" would express the idea he wished to convey—so he gave it up.

Aunt Mary could guess pretty well what was passing in Robert's mind; but as she did not wish to enter into conversation upon *that* subject, she encouraged Robert in a general way to try and be a good boy, when he returned home, and then began to talk of something else.

"I will be a good boy to-day," said Robert to himself, the morning after his return from his Aunt Mary's. "I will try to be as good a boy at home as I am when at Aunt Mary's."

Robert had an irritable temper. A trifle would make him angry, and then would come an outburst of passion. These fits of passion were met by those reproofs which were administered in such a manner, and with such tones of voice, that they certainly seemed to Robert more like scolding than like anything else; and were by no means calculated to restore calmness to his irritated feelings.

Robert was aware of his weakness, and knew if he wished to be a good boy that day he must set a double watch upon his temper. This he tried to do.

The morning was not far advanced, however, before his brother, next older than himself, said something which vexed Robert very much. His eye kindled, his cheeks were flushed, and on his tongue was the angry retort. But just then he thought of his morning's resolution, and with a mighty effort forced back the burning words.

Robert instinctively turned to his mother, to see if the conflict and the victory had been observed by her; but no word or glance of hers gave any intimation that she had taken note of the moral conflict which had been transpiring close by her side, or of the moral victory that had been achieved. Yet she had seen it all. She heard the remark of George, and knowing the irritable temper of Robert, had expected an outburst of passion; but, as it did not occur, she merely congratulated herself that she had not, as she expected, been annoyed by an angry altercation between her sons, and dismissed the subject from her thoughts.

Robert felt disappointed and discouraged. He could could but say to himself, "If Aunt Mary were here, she might not have said a word; but the very glance of her eye would have said as plainly as words could do, 'I understand it all, Robert. You have done bravely. I know you have had a hard battle, and I congratulate you most heartily for the victory you have gained.'"

How amply would Robert have been rewarded by such a smile of approbation for all it had cost him to suppress his angry feelings; and how would his soul have been strengthened for another conflict!

But did not his mother know that it had cost her son something to control his temper, and keep back the angry words which had all but escaped? Could she not read the language of that flashing eye and flushed face, and could she not know that there was a work for her to do even when reproof and condemnation were not called for?

Robert did not *reason* very deeply on the subject, but he felt that if it was right for his mother to condemn when he did wrong, it was no more than right that she should *observe* and approve when he did right. But, though discouraged, and feeling much like a soldier fighting alone, he resolved to persevere yet longer, and see if he could not be a good boy all that day.

An hour or two more passed. Robert had taken out his building blocks, and was very busily engaged in erecting a building, upon which he was bestowing a good deal of thought and contrivance. It was nearly completed, and he was just about to call his mother's attention to it, and ask if he had not done well, when his little sister, in playing about the room, chanced to upset a chair, which, in falling, upset in its turn the building Robert was so carefully rearing. Robert felt very angry—so angry that he even raised his hand to strike his little sister. But again he thought of his morning's resolution, and immediately girded himself to the great work of ruling his own spirit. It was a hard-fought battle, but Robert was conqueror. The uplifted hand fell gently by his side, and not even an angry word escaped him.

His mother was sitting near, engaged with a book. When Robert's edifice fell, she was disturbed with the thought, "Now we shall have a storm!" but when all passed off quietly, and the expected storm did not come, she resumed her reading with a feeling of satisfaction that the affair had passed off so smoothly, but without bestowing one approving glance upon the moral hero who stood in her presence, although that hero was her own son.

Robert was discouraged from continuing the unaided struggle. He had spent, as it were, all his moral courage in this last conflict, and all he had gained, as respected his mother, was freedom from reproof. The next time he was tempted, he yielded almost without a struggle. His mother's reproof, which, as usual, followed instantly upon the offence, stung him to the quick. He felt as if he were the injured party.

"I have tried all day," he said to himself, "to be a good boy, and mother has taken no notice of it. I did not speak angrily to George, this morning, when he provoked me so; and I said not a word to Lucy for her knocking down my house, but mother never so much as smiled upon me, when I was trying to be good; but if I get angry ever so little, I hear of it quickly enough.'"

The more Robert thought of these things, the more

out of temper he grew. He did not any longer try to control himself, but all the rest of the day was so peevish, it was hardly safe to speak to him.

Now it was not from any want of love for her son that Mrs. Molton erred so greatly in her management of him. As Robert had said, she loved him well enough to do almost anything for him; but she did not cultivate a hearty sympathy with him. "What if his sister did throw down his play-house? It was *only* a play-house, a very small thing to be angry about, and he did not deserve much credit for not getting angry about such a trifle."

Now this reasoning was wrong, all wrong. If this mother had placed herself back to the days of her own early childhood, and candidly asked herself how she would *then* have felt about the very same thing, she would have felt that it was *not* a trifle to Robert, and she would have learned an invaluable lesson of sympathy for her child in his childish struggles, conflicts, and victories.

The exhibition of such sympathy was just what Robert needed to encourage him in the efforts which he really did often make to overcome his faults. All he asked was that these efforts should be appreciated. A smile of approbation, as the reward of one such successful effort as Robert had made that day, would have done more to aid him to overcome his violent temper than all the reproofs he had ever received.

"Have you come to a decision, Mrs. Bradford?"

"Yes, sir." This was meant to be firmly spoken; but there was a low tremor in the soft, sad voice of the pale young woman, in widow's weeds, who answered, that betrayed more feeling than she wished to manifest.

"You will let Edward come?"

"Excuse me, sir, I—I—"

"Oh, very well! very well!" said the visiter, in an impatient tone of voice. "Just as you please, ma'am." And he arose quickly, and commenced buttoning his coat across his breast. "It's a matter of indifference to me—wholly so. As an old friend of Mr. Bradford's, I thought it but right to make this offer for the benefit of his son. Not that it is of any special importance to me; for I can have my pick of a dozen lads quite as bright as your boy, and as well suited for my purpose. To Edward I have given the preference, out of regard to his father. You decline my offer to take him, and that ends the matter. I have done my duty."

Mr. Gardiner—that was the man's name—turned partly away, and made a step towards the door. Mrs. Bradford, instead of seeking to prevent his abrupt departure, shrunk deeper in the chair that supported her slender person. How strong a contrast presented between the two! one a stout, confident, easy-to-do in the world, self-reliant man; the other a weak, almost friendless, sad and desponding woman.

With his hand upon the door, Mr. Gardiner paused, and looked back, half proudly, upon the sorrowing widow of his early friend, whose eyes, cast down, ventured not to meet his gaze.

"Think again, ma'am," said he coldly, almost severely.

"I have thought it all over, Mr. Gardiner," was answered in a firmer voice than the man expected to hear. At the same moment the eyes of Mrs. Bradford were lifted to his face. Steadily she gazed, until his eyes fell to the floor.

"I *have* thought it all over," she repeated, "and my decision has not been made without a long and painful struggle. For your kind preference, believe me. I am grateful; and I thank you for it in the name of him who, when living, you called your friend. But I cannot accept the advantage you offer my son."

"Good morning, ma'am." The words were said abruptly, almost rudely. A moment after, and the door closed heavily.

"Mother," said a lad, who, until now, had remained a silent observer of what passed between his mother and her visiter, "why won't you let me go to Mr. Gardiner's? I'm sure he offered us very fair. Three dollars a week for the first year; and after that as much more as I might be worth to him. That was what he said."

Edward had come to the side of his mother; and stood looking quite soberly into her face. It was clear, from the tone of his voice, that he was not pleased with her decision.

"I don't believe I'll ever have as good an offer again

He wanted me, and said he'd do well by me," added the boy, pettishly.

"I have not declined this proposition of Mr. Gardiner's without good reason, Edward." Mrs. Bradford spoke with gentle earnestness, and there were tears in her eyes as she lifted them to the fine, manly face of her son.

"I'll never have another chance like this," said Edward.

"A chance for what?" asked his mother.

"Mr. Gardiner is a rich man," said the boy.

"I know he is," was answered.

"He's doing a large business."

"Yes."

"And he promised to do well by me."

"He did. And yet, Edward, it was best for me to decline his offer; and the day will come, I trust, when you will see this as clearly as I do."

The boy was far from being satisfied. The necessity for entering upon some employment was imperative; that he clearly understood, and his mind was made up to do his part bravely. Two places were offered for his acceptance, one in the large wholesale store of Mr. Gardiner, and the other in the counting-room of a Mr. Lee, a young man of small means, who had just started a commission business. Mr. Lee could offer no salary for the first year; and this was a serious drawback, for Mrs Bradford's income was exceedingly limited—insufficient, in fact, for the comfortable maintenance of herself and son.

In deciding between the two situations offered to

Edward, she had suffered a strong conflict. The fairest promise of worldly advantage for her son was on the side of the rich merchant; but she had no confidence in his principles. That he lacked integrity of character, and, in business, was guilty of practices which her clear sense of what was right between man and man hesitated not to class as dishonest actions, she knew through her husband, who had become attached to him early in life, but in later years had withdrawn himself from an intimate association.

James Lee was the younger brother of a very dear friend, and a man of different stamp from Gardiner. He had been carefully educated—morally as well as intellectually—and bore the reputation, among all with whom he had any intercourse, of a just man. This was the reason why Mrs. Bradford decided to place Edward in his care, instead of accepting the more advantageous offer of Mr. Gardiner. In looking to the future of her child, she had a regard for something more permanent, more to be desired, and more soul-satisfying, than wealth or position. Of all things, she wished to see him grow up a true man. Not a mere self-seeker; not one who, to elevate himself, would coldly tread down the weak, or wrong the helpless and ignorant. She had tried to make Edward comprehend the wide difference between the characters of these two men, and the great injury he might sustain in coming under the influence and control of Mr. Gardiner. But Edward saw only the worldly advantage that was promised, and perceived in his mother's objections only idle fears.

Thus was Mrs. Bradford's trial made only the more

severe. If there had been cheerful, or even dutiful
acquiescence on the part of her son, her feelings on the
occasion would have been of a less painful character.
But she was resolute. The place offered by Mr. Lee
was accepted, and Edward entered his counting-room,
simply in obedience to his mother's wishes.

When it became known among the friends of Mrs.
Bradford that she had refused to let Edward go into
Mr. Gardiner's store, she was severely blamed. A bro
ther of her late husband said many harsh things to her
on the subject; and some that she felt to be insulting.
But she did not waver, even though family estrange-
ments followed, and she was left still more alone in the
world.

One of the false views of life which Mrs. Bradford
had now, under the teaching of stern necessity, to un-
learn, was, that for a woman to work for money had in
it something degrading. From childhood up to this
period, all things needful for life and comfort had been
provided for her by the hands of others. Father and
husband had kept her above the sphere of care as to
what we shall eat, or what we shall drink, or wherewithal be clothed; and insensibly she had come to feel
something like contempt for all women who were compelled to toil for the bread that perisheth.

How all was changed now! The mother's pure love
lifted her out of this obscurity, and she saw a meaning
in the words that pronounced him greatest of all who
became servant of all, that never before came even dimly
to her perceptions. All hopes, all aspirations, all purposes in life, were now terminated in the future welfare

of her son; and for his sake she was ready to do and sacrifice all that a true and loving heart can do and sacrifice in this world.

As Edward would receive nothing for the first year, and as the meagre remnant of property that survived to her after the settlement of her husband's estate was insufficient for the support of herself and son, Mrs. Bradford now began to revolve in her mind the ways and means of procuring an additional income

"What shall I do?" How earnestly, even tearfully, did she ask this question! How earnestly and tearfully is it daily asked by thousands, who, like Mrs. Bradford, are thrown upon the world, and made wholly dependent on their feeble resources! Yet to whom comes a clear, confident answer?

The education of Mrs. Bradford had not been thorough. A little of almost everything taught in fashionable schools she had learned; yet nothing had been so fully acquired as to give her a teacher's proficiency. She had a fair acquaintance with French, and could speak it with some fluency; but possessed no critical knowledge of the language. She could draw tolerably well; but had no taste for the beautiful art. For years her music had been neglected. So far, therefore, as her early education was concerned, it availed her little or nothing in the present trying position of affairs.

"What shall I do?" How sadly, almost hopelessly, over and over again did Mrs. Bradford repeat these words! and yet there was not even an echo to the question.

One day it was mentioned in her presence that the

matron of a certain charitable institution had resigned her place, and that the Board of Directors were about appointing another. It flashed through her mind that here was a chance for her; but with the thought pride awoke, and her cheeks burned as she imagined herself in the position of a matron where she had once been a lady patroness. For a time she shrunk away into herself, and pushed the thought afar off. But turn which way she would, no light from any other quarter broke through the clouds that gathered above her, black as midnight.

Nearly a month had gone by since Edward entered the counting-room of Mr. Lee. From the beginning he had looked sober and seemed spiritless. To him the present was cheerless, and the future lured him on with no bright promise. A school companion, named Henry Long, had obtained the situation with Mr. Gardiner, and it so happened that the two lads met almost every day. Their conversation naturally turned upon their relative positions; and the contrasts which were drawn, always left Edward's mind in a state of dissatisfaction. The business of Mr. Gardiner was very heavy, his employees numbering over one hundred; while in the store and counting-room of Mr. Lee were only Edward and a porter. Mr. Lee kept his own books; Mr. Gardiner was, moreover, a "liberal" man—generous towards his clerks, and not over particular in regard to them, provided they were always in place and active during business hours. There was in the whole operations of his large establishment, an imposing progression, which, in contrast with the intermitting and lighter operations of the young commission merchant, made the latter appear in the eye of Edward, almost contemptible.

He came home one evening, after one of his talks with Henry Long, considerably fretted at what he chose to think the great injustice practised by his mother in refusing to let him accept the place which had been offered by Mr. Gardiner. On that very day, a favourable answer had been received by Mrs. Bradford to her application for the situation of matron in an Orphan Asylum.

She had not spoken to Edward on the subject, and he had no suspicion of what was in her mind. How to break it to him, was now the subject of her thoughts. That he would oppose her, she knew; and the more strongly, because it involved the breaking up of their home. And was it just to him for her to do so? That was still a question, ever recurring, though answered over and over again—conclusively, the mother *tried* to think.

Edward came in with his usual quiet step. There was no smile on his lip as he glanced into his mother's face; and though she tried to smile an evening welcome home, there was only a feeble ray upon her countenance that soon faded.

"Edward," said Mrs. Bradford, as they were about leaving the tea-table, almost compelling herself to introduce a subject that could no longer be kept back,—" we shall have to make a change in our mode of life."

The boy looked at her inquiringly.

"I need not say, my son, that we are very poor," she added; "too poor even to maintain our present style of living."

"Well, mother, whose fault is it?" Edward spoke coldly—nay, severely.

"I do not charge it as the fault of any one," answered Mrs. Bradford.

"I do, then," was the quick response. Accusation and rebuke, both, were in the boy's tones.

"Upon whom?" The mother looked him firmly in the face.

"It is your fault," said he.

"Edward!"

"I cannot help it, mother. But for your refusal to let me accept the offer of Mr. Gardiner, I might now be receiving three dollars weekly, which would help a great deal."

"In that small gain would have been, I fear, the seed of an infinite loss, my son." The voice of Mrs. Bradford trembled, and her eye grew suddenly dim.

"Uncle Bradford said that was all a woman's silly notion, and I believe him."

Edward uttered this with a cruel thoughtlessness, and his words pierced the heart of his mother. A little while she looked with a rapidly changing countenance into his face—looked half timidly, but oh! so sorrowfully; and then leaning down until her forehead rested upon the table at which she sat, sobbed out loudly, while her body shook as with a convulsion.

Touched, but not subdued by this effect of his hard words, Edward arose and commenced walking the room hurriedly. Gradually Mrs. Bradford regained possession of her feelings, and, in a few minutes, was able to command her voice entirely.

"I have looked to your good alone, my son," said she; "and time will prove that I did not err in accepting the place you have, instead of the one offered by Mr. Gardiner. Do your mother at least the justice to believe that she was governed by no selfish consideration. But to recur to what I wished to say in the beginning. We are too poor to retain even this humble home. Providentially, however, in this our extremity, a way has been opened. This afternoon I received notice that I was appointed matron in the ——— Orphan Asylum. The salary is five hundred dollars."

Edward's face flushed suddenly, and then grew pale as ashes. He had continued walking the floor with uneasy step, but now he stood still, gazing upon his mother with a strange, doubting, startled look.

"With this income," she added, "and no expense of rent or housekeeping, I shall be able to support you comfortably, until your services in Mr. Lee's counting-room command a salary. The only drawback in the matter is the giving up of our home."

The whole manner of the boy underwent a change. Without speaking, he moved across the room to where his mother still sat, and, bending down, laid his head upon her bosom, and burst into tears. Not only was his pride wounded at the thought of her taking the place of a matron in an orphan asylum; he was touched by so strong a manifestation of her self-sacrificing love for him. And he had, moreover, an oppressive sense of loneliness——home-sickness it might almost be called—as the idea of separation from his mother presented itself vividly.

"You will not go there, dear mother," he sobbed, lifting his tearful face from her bosom.

"It would be wrong, under present circumstances, for me to refuse the offer," was the quiet answer.

"You cannot do it—you must not do it, mother!" Edward spoke with rising warmth.

"There is no alternative, my son."

"Don't say so, mother. Wait, wait."

"Wait for what, Edward?"

"I can, I will earn something. I must support you, not you support me. My hands are ready, and my heart willing. No—no—you shall not go there."

"Mr. Lee cannot pay you a salary at present."

"Then I must find some one who can," was the resolute answer.

"I do not wish you to leave Mr. Lee's service. I know it will be best for you in the end to remain with him," interposed Mrs. Bradford.

"I cannot work, starving," said the lad, bitterly.

"Calm yourself, Edward." The mother spoke earnestly and tenderly. "Trust something in my judgment. Time will prove to you that I am right in what I propose doing."

"Right to take from me my home?" said the boy, with a mournfulness in his voice that thrilled on his mother's heart-strings, and started in her mind a new train of thoughts. Yes, it would be taking from him his home, poor and humble though it was; for when she entered upon the matron's duties, he would go among strangers; and who could tell whether the new relations into which he must come, would be for good or evil?

And now Mrs. Bradford's purpose, so firmly settled, began to waver.

'You have not yet accepted the offer?" inquired Edward, after his excitement of feeling had in a measure subsided, and thought began to flow on in a clearer current.

"No, but I will be expected to give an answer at once."

"Can it be put off until the day after to-morrow?"

"It might."

"Then don't say yes, to-morrow; don't, mother! Promise me, won't you?"

"But what will it avail, my son?"

"Only wait, mother," urged the lad eagerly. "Say that you will wait."

"I need not give the answer to-morrow; and if you so earnestly desire it, I will not."

Edward said no more, but from that moment his thoughts were indrawn, and he remained during the evening in a state of deep distraction. All the powers of his young mind he was taxing for a solution of one of life's intricate problems. He was in a more tranquil, hopeful state on the next morning; for he had come to a decision, and that was, to tell the story of his mother's extremity, and ask from Mr. Lee either the payment of a salary, or a release from his engagement.

Mr. Lee heard his story, and it awakened a strong interest in favour of the lad, for he was a man of generous sympathies. But the question of paying Edward a salary was one that he could not easily decide. His business was only in its forming stage, and in commencing it, he had graduated his expenses to the very lowest scale. It was part of his calculation to do without a clerk for the first year; and to take an office boy, who would be compensated for his services during at least that period by the knowledge of business he would acquire. This economical arrangement of his affairs was not, in any sense, the offspring of mean cupidity; nor was it grounded in a principle of injustice to others. It was only a measure of prudence, the dictate of a clear judgment. "Little boats keep near the shore," was one of his safe axioms.

"I will think about this, Edward," he answered, kindly, after the boy had told his story, "and see what can be done. I like your manly spirit, and right feeling towards your mother."

There was something so cheerful and encouraging in Mr. Lee's voice, that the lad felt his heart bound with hope. The fact was, on this very morning, the young commission merchant had received a letter from a large manufacturing establishment at the East, notifying him of a handsome consignment of goods, and promising to keep him supplied. The goods were in demand, and sales could be made to some of the best houses in the city. From this source alone, his profits would be several hundred dollars in the year.

Mr. Lee was not one of those men whose sympathy for others grows narrower, as the dawn of a more prosperous day begins to break along the murky horizon.

"I am glad for his sake, as well as for my own," was the thought which flitted through his mind, after Edward had told his story, "that a favourable change in business prospects has just occurred. I can now afford to pay him something; and I will do it. A lad with such a spirit deserves encouragement."

As Edward was about leaving the counting-room at dinner-time, Mr. Lee said to him,

"I have been thinking over what you told me this morning, and I have every disposition to meet your wishes. My business, as you know, is yet small, and the income from it limited. But I have just received some better consignments, with the promise of liberal shipments of goods, from a large manufactory. Yesterday, I do not think your application would have met with a favourable answer. Now I can offer you a salary of one hundred and fifty dollars for the first year."

Tears sprung to the lad's eyes, and he could not restrain the impulse that prompted him to seize the hand of Mr. Lee.

"Oh! I am so glad!" he exclaimed, as a light broke over his face.

"But that sum," added Mr. Lee, "will not go far towards supporting yourself and mother."

"Mother has a small income; and this will help very much. I think she can make it do."

Mr. Lee mused for some moments.

"I've been thinking since you spoke to me this morning—"

Mr. Lee paused, and seemed turning something over in his mind, that was not altogether clear to him.

"I've been thinking, perhaps, you might do something for yourself," he at length said.

Edward's face brightened.

"There are some little articles in which you might

trade safely. In breaking bales of goods, for instance, pieces of rope and bagging accumulate. For these odds and ends there is a sale. I know two or three stores where you can buy the article, and I know where you can sell it at a small advance. It will take so small a portion of your time and attention that I can have no objection, and the matter is so simple and safe that you will run no risk."

The light faded from the boy's face; observing which, Mr. Lee said,

"It does not strike you favourably."

"I have no money to buy with," was the dispirited answer.

"Oh, as to that," came the cheerful response, "no very large capital will be required. Ten or fifteen dollars will start you in the business, and I can supply that."

"You are very kind, sir," was Edward's grateful answer. A few moments he stood with his eyes bent upon the floor—then moving away he left the counting-room, and hurried home to communicate the good news to his mother. As he ascended the stairs, leading to the apartments they occupied, he heard the voice of a man in his mother's room, and on opening the door, his eyes fell upon the cold face of his Uncle Bradford. A brief and distant greeting took place, and then the visitor said to the widow of his brother,

"The salary is a liberal one, and will make you very comfortable. I am glad you were so fortunate as to secure the appointment. You may not know that you are in a good measure indebted to me for your success. I made interest for you in an influential quarter."

"Mother is not going there," said Edward, abruptly. He was unable to keep back the words that leaped to his tongue.

Mr. Bradford turned suddenly upon the boy, and scowled darkly.

"Not going where," he asked.

"Not going to be a matron in an orphan asylum," answered Edward, firmly.

"She isn't, ha!" Mr. Bradford's lip had a sneer upon it; and he looked first at the boy and then at his mother.

"No, sir, she isn't going." And Edward stood up and returned the gaze of his uncle with so steady a look, that Mr. Bradford felt irritated beyond measure.

"Oh, very well," said he, in an offended voice—"very well—if you are master here, I have nothing to say." And he arose, and took two or three hurried steps across the room. At the door he paused and glanced back towards Mrs. Bradford, who looked bewildered, and almost frightened at the unexpected rencontre, so to speak, between Edward and his uncle.

"It's no use, I find," said he, speaking severely, "for me to try to do anything for you. My advice has not been taken in a single instance since my brother's death; and now I shall just let you go your own way. You were silly enough to refuse Mr. Gardiner's excellent offer to take Edward. There isn't a more advantageous place in the city—his fortune would have been made

I'm out of all patience with you! But, gang y'r ain gait—gang y'r ain gait! It will be all the same to me. And just bear this in mind—don't call on me to help you out of any of the troubles your stupidity may create."

And Mr. Bradford went off in a passion, leaving the widow in tears.

"Don't cry, mother dear—don't cry," said Edward, tenderly, coming to the side of his weeping parent, and laying his face to hers. "You're not going to the Asylum. Mr. Lee says he will pay me one hundred and fifty dollars for the first year, and that is as much as Mr. Gardiner promised. He spoke very kindly to me; and said he would show me how I could trade a little for myself, and make a few dollars now and then. Oh, mother! I feel such a weight taken from my heart."

Mrs. Bradford could not answer in words, but she drew the boy's face tightly to her breast, and kissed over and over again, fervently, his pure white forehead.

"Mr. Lee is a true man," she said, when she could trust herself to speak. "He is not rich, like Mr. Gardiner; but he has a larger heart, my son."

Edward raised himself up, and looked earnestly at his mother. Her words seemed to have light in them, and made things clear which were before in obscurity.

"A kind, true heart, Edward," the mother added, "is worth more than gold; and you can trust it better."

"Mr. Lee has a kind, true heart," said the lad, speaking as if to himself.

"That I have known for years, Edward," answered his mother; "and he has not only a true heart, but just and honourable principles. It was for this reason that I decided against Mr. Gardiner and in his favour. I knew it would be better for you in the end to be under his care; and, already, this is becoming apparent even in your eyes."

Serious thought was now given by Mrs. Bradford to the subject of accepting or declining the appointment which she had just received. Would it be right for her, under the circumstances, to refuse an offer of five hundred dollars a year? Another such opportunity would hardly again occur. If she did refuse, the act would estrange certain friends who had interested themselves in her behalf; and in case of future extremity, no dependence could be placed on their kind offices. As these and other considerations were revolved, her mind came into a bewildered state; and she was sorely oppressed by doubts. Edward opposed her acceptance, and begged her not to take from him his home, humble and obscure though it might be.

"I will live in a garret with you, mother," he said. "Anywhere—I will be contented with poor food and plain clothing, until I grow older."

If the thought of Mrs. Bradford had in any respect turned inwards upon herself—if, in thinking of a clear income of five hundred dollars a year, her imagination had pictured a condition of freedom from care and worldly anxieties, every selfish impulse was stifled now. "What will be best for my boy?" That was the earnestly asked question, and upon that turned a decision of the case. Clearly, now, she saw the dangers to which Edward would be exposed, if removed from her loving care—her watchful guardianship—and she wondered within herself that this had not vividly presented itself before.

"We will remain together, my son," were her calmly spoken words, after all was decided in her mind; "and if we can only get bread to eat and water to drink, we will share them, and be thankful that the worse evil of separation is yet far from us."

Both mother and son had passed through what to them was a fiery trial, but now they saw with a purer vision; now they felt stronger to endure, and had a better hope for the future.

When the purpose of Mrs. Bradford was made known to her friends, and they became aware of the slender support she had chosen, instead of the comfortable income which had been offered for her acceptance, they were greatly displeased, and censured her strongly; even going so far as to charge her with lack of energy, and insinuating that both pride and indolence had conspired to effect her decision. She bore the storm meekly, for she knew that the words of self-justification she could speak would not be understood. Estrangement from her husband's relations was the consequence, and an almost total exclusion from the old social circles.

Patiently and hopefully she bore all this, for her earnest, self-devoted love for Edward gave clearness to her vision, and she saw that she was moving in the right way. Very poorly did they live on their slender income, but day after day was the widow's heart made glad by the knowledge that her son was gradually learning to estimate truly the character of Mr. Lee, and to imbibe from him those higher principles of action by which his own life was governed. True to his promise to Edward, the latter had not only advanced him a small sum of money to purchase certain articles in which he might freely traffic, but had advised him where and how to buy, and where to sell. From this source the lad was soon in receipt of light profits, that were never, from the beginning, less than five or six dollars a month; all of which was given to his mother.

One evening Edward said to his mother, "Henry Long told me something about Mr. Gardiner, to-day, that don't seem to me just right. I'm sure Mr. Lee wouldn't have done such a thing."

"What was it, my son?" asked Mrs. Bradford.

"Henry, in looking over an account which a merchant from the country had just settled, discovered an error of a hundred dollars against the merchant. He showed it to Mr. Gardiner, saying, as he did so, ' Mr. —— told us that he wouldn't leave until six o'clock this afternoon. Shall I go round to the hotel, and see him about it?'

"'No!' was Mr. Gardiner's answer. 'Let him find it out himself, which he will do, if he is sharp enough; and if he is not, he deserves to lose it.'"

"That is dishonest," said Mrs. Bradford, with much gravity of manner.

"So I told Henry; but he laughed, and said Mr. Gardiner was keen, and knew how to take care of number one."

"And did Henry Long make so light of a wicked action? I thought better of him than that, my son.'

"He wouldn't have made light of it, I am sure, when we went to school together. Then he was a very honourable boy."

"Evil communications corrupt good manners. There must, then, be something wrong in his associations."

"I'm afraid so," said Edward.

"Does it not occur to you in what direction this may lie?"

Edward looked thoughtful.

"If a man in Mr. Gardiner's position makes light of dishonesty, is there not danger in coming within the sphere of his influence? If the principal in a large establishment manifests no just regard for the rights of others, what is to be expected from his subordinates? Believe me, Edward, there is great danger in being in the service of such a man. And now I am sure you can begin to see how grave my reasons were for not permitting you to accept the offer he seemed so kindly to make."

What a glow of pleasure warmed the bosom of Mrs. Bradford, as her son expressed strongly his abhorrence of Mr. Gardiner's principles, and said that he hoped ever to be thankful that he had a mother who was wise enough to save him from the influences of such a man!

Time passed on. Mr. Lee's business steadily increased, though not rapidly. He was active, prompt, and honourable in dealing, thus securing a good reputation in business circles. At the end of a year he was able to increase Edward's salary to three hundred dollars, and so intelligent had the lad become in such matters of trade as were permitted to him on his own account, that he added two hundred dollars to this income during the second year he was with the young commission merchant. From this time the widow and her son, though still in obscurity, and overlooked by friends who should have stood by them in their hours of need, and encouraged them as they passed through the trials of adversity, had not only all things needful for comfort, but enjoyed a measure of happiness that is meted out to but few.

The years now glided by with a fleeter motion. Mr. Lee's business steadily increased. His strictly honourable dealings had become widely known; and every season he received new and more valuable consignments. For Edward he had from the beginning felt a true interest. Very careful was he to instil just principles into his mind, and to demonstrate the fallacy of the bad maxim, so widely prevalent, that no man can conduct business successfully at the present day and be strictly honest. Success, he always maintained, was dependent on a thorough knowledge of the business in which a man engaged, united with untiring industry. "This," he would say, "is the only safe road in which to walk All others are full of danger." Every year he continued to increase the salary of Edward; for every year he became of more value to him.

It was just seven years from the day on which Mrs. Bradford declined the offer of the rich merchant to take her son into his service. Circumstances were considerably altered. Edward's salary was enabling her to live in more comfort, and some of her old friends were beginning to approach again. Of these was the mother of Henry Long, the boy who had taken the place at

Mr. Gardiner's. Henry had grown up a gay, dashing young man; and it was plain to all close observers that in his contact with the world he had soiled his garments.

Mrs. Long, rather a worldly-minded woman herself, did not seem clearly conscious of the change for the worse that was steadily progressing. Henry had a manly, confident way about him that gratified her vanity; and he adroitly deceived her in many things that a truer-hearted woman would have known by an unerring instinct. Mrs. Long had called twice upon Mrs. Bradford; and the latter, who did not much care to renew the acquaintance, felt that it was hardly kind not to return a visit. So, one fine morning she rung the bell at Mrs. Long's door. The servant who admitted her had a frightened look, and exclaimed, as soon as the door was closed, "Oh, ma'am, go up quickly to Mrs. Long! I don't know what ails her!"

"Is she sick?" was Mrs. Bradford's anxious inquiry.

"Something's the matter. She's in a dreadful way," answered the servant. "A man left a letter for her just now, and as soon as she began to read it she turned as pale as death, and fell right down on the floor. I got her on the bed, and she's lying there now, moaning and crying, oh, so dreadfully! Do go up, and see her. I don't know what to do!"

Mrs. Bradford went hastily up to the chamber of Mrs. Long. As she opened the door, the groans that fell upon her ears were so full of anguish that every nerve thrilled with pain. Crouching down upon the bed, with her face pressed into and hidden on a pillow, lay the friend she had called to visit, shivering as if in a strong ague-fit. Going quickly to the bedside, she placed her hand upon Mrs. Long, and repeated her name. The suffering woman did not seem to feel the touch, nor hear the voice.

"Mrs. Long! Mrs. Long!" The call was repeated in a low, earnest, penetrating voice; but the only response was a moan more full of anguish.

"My friend! Mrs. Long!"

It availed not. Her ears seemed deaf—her senses all indrawn.

"What great trouble has come upon you so suddenly, my friend?" Very tenderly did Mrs. Bradford speak, bending her face low to the ear of the wretched woman. There was a half-smothered murmur of words.

"It is Mrs. Bradford," said the visiter.

The hands of Mrs. Long were instantly waved backward, with a repelling motion.

"Think of me as a true friend—as an earnest, sympathizing friend."

"Mother! mother! send for my mother!" was the sufferer's answer. And again she waved her hand for Mrs. Bradford to leave her.

Delicacy forbade further intrusion on the part of Mrs. Bradford. Leaving the room, she made known the wish of Mrs. Long to have her mother, who lived near by, sent for, and went back to her own home deeply pained at the scene she had witnessed, and wondering what it could mean.

When Edward came home that evening, he said to his mother, the moment he entered,

"A dreadful thing has happened here, to-day!"

"What?" was the quick inquiry.

"Henry Long sailed in the English steamer at twelve o'clock, after having robbed his employer of more than a hundred thousand dollars."

"Oh, no, Edward! Impossible!"

"It is too true."

"But he could not abstract so much money at one time?"

"No; but the frauds on the house have been going on, as is alleged, for years. This morning he was sent to collect some large drafts, and make heavy deposits, the whole amounting to over forty thousand dollars. Instead of making the deposits, he bought bills of exchange, and left for Europe in the steamer."

"Dreadful! Dreadful!"

"In consequence of this large abstraction of money, Mr. Gardiner was unable to meet his payments, to-day, and called a hurried meeting of creditors. We had sold him some goods, and Mr. Lee was present at the meeting. And, what do you think he says? Why, that it is the strong impression of nearly all his creditors, after hearing his story, that he is a partner in the guilt of his clerk."

"Oh, Edward! Edward!"

A shade of fear went darkly over the mother's face, as she remembered how near she had been to yielding to the strong pressure that was on her, and consenting that her son should take the place afterwards filled by Henry Long. "Thanks to my Heavenly Father, for giving me the strength to endure!" was her fervent heart-ejaculation.

"The failure, that comes in consequence of Henry's crime, will be a very bad one. False entries were exhibited (too quickly discovered, some think,) showing the abstraction of over sixty thousand dollars, besides the heavy sum taken to-day. If the creditors get thirty cents in the dollar, it will be a large dividend on the effects produced by Mr. Gardiner."

"Then he may be a worse man than his absconding clerk."

"And no doubt is, mother. He has not, for some time, borne a good reputation among honourable business men. I have heard the worst epithets applied to him by merchants."

"Oh, Edward!" said Mrs. Bradford, speaking with so much feeling that tears stood in her eyes, "how thankful I am that you did not enter his service instead of Henry Long!"

"Not more thankful than I am," was the reply of Edward. "For years I have seen how wisely you acted in choosing a place for me with a true, good man, instead of one whose only recommendation was the worldly advantage he had to offer. How far I might have been corrupted in his service I know not—but I have, several times to-day, had an inward shudder as I thought of it.'

There was a pause, and then the young man said, with a brightening countenance,

"But I have some good as well as evil tidings for your ear. Mr. Lee has offered me an interest in his business on most liberal terms; and I have accepted the proposition."

Mrs. Bradford's face kindled with a glow of delight. No strong expression of pleasure leaped from her tongue; she only clasped the hand of her son, and looking at him with an expression of maternal love and pride, said,

"I have my reward, and it comes quicker and more abundant than ever imagination realized. My dearest hope for you in life has been that you might be a true-hearted, honourable, honest man. You are all this, Edward!—all this. And now there is added the worldly prosperity that I was willing to sacrifice for those higher and better things. There is no happier mother in the land this day. My cup runs over!"

FITS OF OBSTINACY.

My memory recalls one morning when, superintending the instruction of a very intelligent and amiable child, a sister about ten years of age, I was surprised at her hesitation in commencing to read some verses of rhyme which I had selected for the purpose. I waited. "Come, Annie!" No answer—a pause. "For what are you waiting?" No reply. "Can't you begin?" I read a verse. "Now, then;" not a sound, but a quiet, undisturbed look, without the appearance of any feeling, but that of a resolute determination *not* to read. If I rightly remember, an hour must have passed without any progress towards the desired end; until at length I said quietly and affectionately, for dearly I loved the little one:—"Annie, I am sorry to see you so naughty and obstinate; you *must* read it, you know," and beginning to read I went through the several verses. "Now, then, like a good child." Annie began, in a somewhat low voice, gradually raising it as she proceeded. A gentle word of commendation cheered her on to the end, when I patted her shoulder, and asked her if she could not read it better with another trial. Annie answered in the affirmative, and went through the task the second time, with her usual accuracy and propriety. The matter had now ended, business proceeded in its ordinary manner, and no allusion was ever made to it afterwards. I never could account for this *fit* of obstinacy. It stood alone in the child's career. Annie remembers not the hour which almost frightened her youthful instructress I have not, however, been so successful in other cases. Permit me to say, that I should hesitate to use expressions of pity and sorrow for the poor little dear that is unable to perform the very easy act. Such a proceeding would *sting* some proud, self-important children, and it would wound some of a tenderly affectionate disposition. It would also probably elicit the thought that you either wanted discernment, of which some would take advantage, or convey an idea that you were deliberately saying what you know to be an untruth. I have sat during one, two, three, or more hours, quietly waiting for the working of a simple sum. I have first pointed out the error, and desired that it should be rectified. "If you do not know the table correctly, get your book and ascertain, but bring me the sum of your own working;" and for this I have waited with as much temper and self-possession as I could possibly command until I obtained it. I do not say I retained my seat the whole time, or that I kept the child in the same room. On the contrary, I have, if the weather were suitable, sent her into the garden, when probably the change in her will might be effected in part by the change of air and scene. But while a little relief was afforded from the close application of the study, and the slate or book laid aside for a short time, no other occupation was allowed till the sum or lesson was accomplished. The hour of repose has occasionally arrived, and brain and body wearied, I have sent the moral patient to bed with some such remark—"to-morrow, the first thing after breakfast, I hope we shall get over this difficulty. It *can* be done, it is *right* it *should* be done, and you know all other business stands still till this shall have been accomplished." Frequently have I alluded to some passage in Holy Writ, as a warning, or a rule, or for encouragement, as the case might seem to require. Patience is the grand requisite, combined with quiet and considerate kindness; but some children make much larger demands upon these qualities in the parent or educator than do others. Verily, mothers work for Eternity, and onerous is the task committed to them.

THE SENSITIVE MOTHER.

"When you are married, Isabel, and have children of your own, you will then know how much I love you."

"I know you love me, dear mother. If I did not acknowledge and understand your love, what should I be but the most ungrateful of living beings?"

"No one who is not a mother herself can rightly understand a mother's love. What you feel for me, and what you fancy I feel for you, comes no nearer the reality, Isabel, than the chirp of the sparrow does to the song of the nightingale. The fondest child does not fully return the love of the coldest mother."

Tears came into Isabel's eyes; for her mother spoke in tender, querulous accents of uncomplaining wrong, which went to the daughter's heart. Mrs. Gray was one of those painfully introspective people who live on themselves; who think no one loves as they love, no one suffers as they suffer; who believe they give their heart's blood to receive back ice and snow, and who pass their lives in agonizing those they would die to benefit. A more lonely-hearted woman never, in her own opinion, existed, although her husband had, she thought, a certain affection from habit for her; but any real heart-sympathy, any love equal to her fond adoration of him, was no more like her own feelings than stars are equal to the noonday sun.

"Not a bad simile, my dear," Mr. Gray once answered, with his pleasant smile, "since the stars are suns themselves; and if we could change our point of view we might find them even bigger and brighter than our own sun. Who knows but, after all, I, who am such a clod compared to you—who am, you say, so cold and unimaginative—that my star is not a bigger, stronger sun than yours?"

His wife gave back a pale smile of patient suffering, and said sadly,

"Ah, Herbert! if you knew what agony I endure when you turn my affection into ridicule, you would surely spare me."

The frank, joyous husband was, as he expressed it, "shut up for the evening." And then Mrs. Gray wept gently, and called herself the "family kill-joy."

With her daughter it was the same. Isabel's whole soul and life were devoted to her mother. She was the centre round which that young existence steadily revolved. The daughter had not a thought of which her mother was not the principal object, not a wish of which her mother was not the actuating spirit; yet Mrs. Gray could never be brought to believe that her daughter's love equalled hers by countless degrees. Isabel worked for her, played to her, read to her, walked with her, lived for her. "Duty, my Isabel, is not love, and I am not blind enough to mistake the one for the other." This was all the reward Isabel received. When she fell in love, as she did with Charles Houghton, Mrs. Gray's happiness was at an end. Henceforth, her life was one long, weak wail of desolation. She was nothing now; her child had cast her out of her heart, and had given the dearest place to another; her own child, her Isabel, her treasure, her life, her soul. Her hour had passed: but even death seemed to have forgotten her. No one loved her now. She was a down-trodden worm; a poor, despised old woman; an unloved, childless widow! Ah! why could she not die? What sin had she committed to be so sorely tried?

Isabel had many sorrowful hours, and held many long debates with her conscience, asking herself more than once whether she ought not to give up her engagement with Charles Houghton if its continuance made her mother so unhappy; also whether the right thing was not always the most painful. But her conscience did not make out a clear case of filial obligation to this extent, for there was a duty due to her betrothed; and Isabel felt she had no right to trifle with any man after having taught him to love her. She owed the first duty to her parents; but she was not free from obligation to her lover; and even for her mother's sake, she must not quite forget this obligation. So her engagement went on, saddened by her mother's complaints.

"My love," said her father, "Houghton has been speaking to me of your marriage, to-day. Come into my study."

Isabel, pale and red by turns, followed her father, dreading both his acquiescence or refusal. In one she heard her mother's sobs, in the other her lover's despair.

"He says, Bell, that you have been engaged above a year. We must not be hard on him. He is naturally desirous to have the affair settled. What do you say? Will a month from this seem to you too soon for your marriage?"

"As you wish, papa," said Isabel, breaking up a spray of honeysuckle.

"No, no, as you wish, my dear child. Do you think you would be happy with Houghton? Have you known him long enough?"

"Yes, papa: but—"

"But what, love?"

"I hesitate to leave mamma," (her head sorrowfully bent down.)

"That is the trial of life, my child," said Mr. Gray, in a low tone; his face full of that quiet sorrow of a firm nature which represses all outward expression, lest it add a double burden on another. "Yet it is one which, by the nature of things, must be borne. We cannot expect to keep you with us always; and, although it will be a dark day to us when you are gone, yet if it is for your happiness, it ought to be so for ours. Tell me, Bell. What answer do you wish me to give?"

"Will he not wait a little time yet?" and the girl crept closer to her father.

"I see I must act without you," he said, smiling and patting her cheek.

"Poor Charles!" she half sighed.

Her father smiled still, but this time rather sadly, and said,

"There, go back to your mother, child. You are a baby yet, and do not know your own mind better than a girl who has to choose between two toys. You do not know which to leave and which to take. I must, it seems, choose for you."

"Oh, papa!"

"Yes—you need not look so distressed. Trust to me, and meanwhile—go; your mother will be weary for you."

Although this little scene had sunk an old sorrow deeper into his heart, Mr. Gray was, when he joined the family, calm, almost merry. He challenged Charles to a game of bowls on the lawn, and ran a race with Isabel round the garden. When he returned to his wife, she told him, pettishly, "that it was a marvel to her how he could be so unfeeling. See how she suffered from this terrible marriage! And yet she had no right to suffer more than he; but," sighed the lady, "no man ever loved as much as woman loves!"

"And don't you think I feel, my dear, because I don't talk? Can you not understand the duty of silence? Complaints may at times be mere selfishness."

He spoke very mournfully. She shook her head. "People who can control themselves so entirely," she said, "have seldom much to control. If you felt as I do about our darling child, you could neither keep silence, nor feign happiness."

Herbert smiled, but made no answer; and Mrs. Gray fairly cried over Isabel's hard fate in having such an indifferent father.

It was all settled; Isabel was to be married in a month's time. Charles mildly complained of the delay, and thought a fortnight ample time for any preparations; but Isabel told him that a month was ridiculously soon, and she wished her father had doubled it; "only I long very much to see Scotland." They were to go to the Highlands to spend their honeymoon.

Mrs. Gray was entirely inconsolable. The poor woman was not well, and her nerves were more than ordinarily irritable. She gave herself a good deal of extra trouble, too, much more than was necessary, and took cold by standing in a draught, cutting out a gown for Isabel; which the maid would have done a great deal better, and would not have complained of the fatigue of standing so long; which Mrs. Gray did all day long. Her cold, and her grief, and her weariness made her the most painful companion; especially to a devoted daughter. She wept day and night, and coughed in the intervals. She did not eat, and answered every one, who pressed any kind of food on her, reproachfully, as if they had insulted her. She slept very little, and denied even that little. She was always languid, and excess of crushed hopes and unrequited affection stimulated her into a fever.

The marriage-day drew nearer. The preparations, plentifully interspersed with Mrs. Gray's sighs, and damped by her tears, savoured less of a wedding than of a funeral, at which Mrs. Gray was chief mourner. The father, on the contrary—to whom Isabel was the only bright spot in life, and who would lose all in losing her—was the gayest of the party. Isabel herself, divided between her lover and her parents, was half distracted with her conflicting feelings, and often wished she had never seen Charles Houghton at all. She told him so once, to his great dismay, after a scene of hysterics and fainting-fits performed by her mother.

It wanted only a week now to the marriage, when Herbert Gray came down to breakfast alone.

"Where is mamma?" asked Isabel.

"She is not well, my dear, and will have breakfast in bed."

"Poor mamma!—how long her cold has continued! What can be done for her?"

"We must send for Doctor Melville, if she does not get better soon. I am quite uneasy about her, and have been so for some time. But she did not wish a physician to be sent for."

"There is no danger?" asked Isabel, anxiously.

Her father did not answer for a moment; then he said, gravely, "She was never strong, and I find her much weakened by her cough."

By this time breakfast was ready, and Isabel prepared to take up her mother's tray. She looked at her father lovingly when she passed him, and turned back at the door and smiled. Then she softly ascended the stairs. A fearful fit of coughing seemed to have been suddenly arrested as she entered her mother's room. She placed the tray gently on the dressing-table.

There was a faint moan; a moan which caused Isabel an agony of terror. On tearing back the curtains, she beheld her mother lying like a corpse—the bed-clothes saturated with blood. At first she thought of murder, and looked wildly around the room, expecting to see some one again clutch at that sacred life; but Mrs. Gray said faintly, "I have only broken a blood-vessel, my love; send for your father." A new nature seemed to be roused in Isabel. Agitated and frightened as she was, a womanly self-possession seemed to give her double power, both of act and vision, and to bury for ever all the child in her heart. She forgot herself. She thought only of her mother, and what would be good for her. As with all strong natures, sympathy took at once the form of help rather than of pity. She rang the bell and called the maid. "Go down and tell my father he is wanted here," she said, quietly. "Mamma is very ill. Make haste and tell my father; but do not frighten him."

She went back to her mother's room, quietly and steadily, without a sign of terror or bewilderment. She washed the blood from her face, gently; and, without raising her head, she drew off the crimsoned cap. Not to shock her father by the suddenness of all the ghastly evidences of danger, perhaps of death, she threw clean linen over the bed, and placed wet towels on her mother's breast. Then, as her father entered, she drew back the curtains, and opened the window, saying softly, "Do not speak loud, dear papa. She has broken a blood-vessel."

Herbert Gray, from whom his daughter had inherited all her self-command, saw at a glance that everything was already done which could be done without professional advice; and, giving his wife's pale cheek a gentle kiss, he left the room, saying simply, "God bless you!" and in less time than many a younger and more active man could have done it, was at Doctor Melville's door.

All this self-possession seemed to Mrs. Gray only intense heartlessness; and she lay there brooding over the indifference of her husband and child with such bitterness, that at last she burst into a fit of hysterical tears, and threw herself into such agitation, that she brought back the bleeding from the ruptured vessel to a more alarming extent than before. She would have been more comforted, ten thousand times, if they had both fallen to weeping and wailing; and had rendered themselves useless by indulgence in grief. Love with her meant pity and caresses.

"Oh, child!" gasped Mrs. Gray, "how little you love me!"

Isabel said nothing for a moment. She kissed her mother's hand; and with difficulty repressed her tears. For it was a terrible accusation, and almost destroyed her calmness. But, fearing that any exhibition of emotion would excite and harm her mother, she pressed back the tears into her inmost heart, and only said, "Dearest mother, you know I love you more than my life!"

But Mrs. Gray was resolved to see in all this calmness, only apathy. She loosened her daughter's hand pettishly, and sobbed afresh. If Isabel had wept a sea of tears, and had run the risk of killing her with agitation, she would have been better pleased than now. Isabel thought her mind was rather affected, and looked anxiously for her father.

"Don't stay with me, Isabel! Go—go—you want to go," sobbed Mrs. Gray, at long, long intervals. "Go to your lover; he is the first consideration now!"

"Dear mamma, why do you say such terrible things?" said the girl, soothingly. "What has come to you?"

"If you loved me," sighed Mrs. Gray, "you would act differently!"

At this moment Herbert Gray and Doctor Melville entered. Having examined the patient, the doctor at once said,

"You have done everything, Miss Isabel, like the

most experienced nurse. You deserve great praise Had you been less capable or less self-possessed, your mother might have lost her life."

He said this to comfort the patient; but she turned away sadly, and murmured,

"My child does not love me; she has done her duty; but duty is not love!"

Mrs. Gray recovered from this phase of her illness only to fall into another more dangerous. In a few weeks she was pronounced in a deep decline, which might last for some years, or be ended in comparatively a few days—one of those lingering and capricious forms of consumption, that keeps every one in a kind of suspense, than which the most painful certainty would be better.

Of course, Isabel's marriage was postponed to an indefinite time, and Charles Houghton murmured sadly, as was natural. He proved to Isabel in the most conclusive logic that the kindest thing she could do for her mother, and the most convincing proof of love she could give her, was to marry him at once, and then she would have a great deal more time to attend on her; for now his visits took up so much time, and all that would be saved. His logic failed; and then he got very angry. So that between her mother and her lover, the girl's life was not spent among roses. She went on, however, doing her duty steadily; turning neither to the right hand nor to the left, but acting as she felt to be right.

Her mother's querulous complaints used always to be most severe after some terrible scene with Charles, when perhaps he had been beseeching Isabel not to kill him with delay.

One day Charles came to the house looking very pale.

"You are ill!" she said, anxiously.

"I am, Isabel, very ill."

She took his hand and caressed it in both her own, looking fondly into his face. He left his hand quite passive. To say the truth frankly, although he looked ill he looked also sulky.

"Can I do anything for you?"

"Everything, Isabel," he said, abruptly—"marry me."

She tried to smile, but her lover's gravity chilled her.

"You can do all for me, and you do nothing."

"I will do all I can. But if a greater duty—"

"A greater duty!" Charles interrupted. "What greater duty can you have than to the man you love, and whose wife you have promised to be?"

"But, Charley, if I were your wife, I should then have, indeed, no greater duty than your happiness. As it is, I have more sacred ties—though none dearer," she added in her gentlest voice.

"I also have superior duties, Isabel."

She started; but after a moment's pause, she said,

"Certainly!" The young man watched her face intently.

"And how will you feel, Isabel, when I place those ties far above your love, and all I owe you, and all that we have vowed together?"

"Nothing unkind towards you, Charles," Isabel

answered, her heart failing her at the accusing tone of her lover's voice.

"But, Isabel, you will not let me go alone!" he cried passionately. "You cannot have the heart to separate from me—perhaps for ever!"

He threw his arms round her.

"Go alone—separate—what do you mean? Are you going anywhere? or are you only trying me?"

"Trying you, my dear Isabel?—no, I am too sadly in earnest!"

"What do you mean, then?" tears filling her eyes.

"You know that my father's affairs have been rather embarrassed lately?"

"No," she said, speaking very rapidly.

"Yes, his West India property is almost a wreck. He has just lost his agent, of yellow fever, and must send out some one immediately to manage the estate. It is all he has to live on, unless he has saved something —and I don't think he has—when he can no longer practise at the bar. It is too important to be lost."

"Well, Charles?"

"I must go."

There was a deep pause. Isabel's slight fingers closed nervously on the hand in hers; she made a movement as if she would have held him nearer to her.

"And now, what will you do, my Isabel? will you suffer me to go alone; will you let me leave you, perhaps for ever—certainly for years—without the chance of meeting you again—and with many chances of death? Will you virtually break your engagement, and give me back my heart, worn and dead, and broken; or will you brave the world with me, become my wife, and share my fortunes ?"

"Charles, how can I leave my mother, when every day may be her last; yet when, by proper care and management, she may live years longer? What can I do?"

"Come with me. Listen to the voice of your own heart, and become my wife."

Isabel sunk back in deep thought.

"No," she whispered, "my mother first of all—before you."

He let her hand fall from his.

"Choose, then," he said coldly.

She clung to him; weeping now and broken. He pressed her to his heart. He believed that he had conquered.

"Choose," he again whispered. "If you have not chosen already," and he kissed her tenderly.

"Oh, Charles! you know how dearly I love you."

At that moment her mother's cough struck her ear. The windows were open, and it sounded fearfully distinct in the still summer air. Isabel shuddered, and hid her face on her lover's shoulder, resting it there for many minutes.

"I have chosen," she then said, after a long, long pause. She lifted her head and looked him in the eyes. Although pale as a marble statue, but quiet and resolved, she never looked so lovely, never so loveworthy. There was something about her very beauty that awed her lover, and something in the very holiness of her nature that humbled and subdued him—only for a moment;

that passed, and all his man's eagerness and strength of will returned, and he would have given his life to destroy the very virtues he reverenced.

He besought her by every tender word love ever framed, to listen to him and to follow him. He painted scenes of such desolation and of such abject misery without her, that Isabel wept. He spoke of his death as certain, and asked how she would feel when she heard of his dying of a broken heart in Jamaica, and how could she be happy again when she had that on her conscience? And although she besought him to spare her, and once was nearly fainting in his arms from excessive emotion, yet he would not; heaping up her pile of woes high and still higher, and telling her throughout all, "that she did not love him now."

After a fearful scene the girl tore herself away; rushing as if for refuge from a tempting angel, and from herself, into her mother's room; busying herself about that sick-bed with even greater care and tenderness than usual.

"You have been a long time away, Isabel," Mrs. Gray said, petulantly.

"Yes; I am very sorry, dearest mamma, I have been detained." Isabel kissed her withered hand.

"Detained—you don't deny it, Isabel."

"I am very sorry."

Tears trembled in her mother's eyes as she murmured, "Sorry!—Don't stay with me, child, if you wish to go. I am accustomed to be alone."

"I entreat you not to think that I wish to leave you for a moment."

"Oh yes, you do, Isabel! I dare say Charles is below stairs—he seems to be always here since I have been ill. You have a great deal to say to him, I am sure."

"I have said all I had to say," answered Isabel quietly.

She was sitting in the shadow of the window curtains, and, as she spoke, she bent her head lower over her work. Her mother did not see the tears which poured down fast from her eyes.

"Oh, then it was Charles who kept you! I can easily understand, my love, the burden I must be to you. I am sure you are very good not to wish me dead—perhaps you do wish me dead, often—I am in your way, Isabel. If I had died, you would have been happily married by this time; for you would not have worn mourning very long, perhaps. Why have I been left so long to be a burden to my family?"

All this, broken up by the terrible cough, and by sobs and tears, Isabel had to bear and to soothe away, when she herself was tortured with real grief.

Charles departed for Jamaica. The thick shadow of absence fell between their two hearts. Henceforth she must live on duty and forget love; now almost hopeless. A stern decree, this, for a girl of nineteen.

For the youth himself, the excitement of the voyage, the novelty of his strange mode of life, and the distractions of business, were all so many healing elements which soon restored peace to his wounded heart. Not that he was disloyal or forgetful of his love, but he was annoyed and angry. He thought that Isabel might have easily left her mother to go with him, and that she was very wrong not to have done so. Between the excitement of new scenes and new amusements, and the excitement of anger and disappointment, Charles Houghton recovered his serenity, and flourished mightily on Jamaica hospitality.

By the end of that year the invalid grew daily weaker and weaker. She could not leave her bed now; and then she could not sit up even; and soon she lay without motion or colour—and then, on the first day of spring she died. She died on the very same day that Charles Houghton entered the house of the rich French planter, Gerard, and was presented to his heiress, Pauline.

Pauline Gerard! a small, dark, gleaming gem, a flitting humming-bird—a floating flower—a fire-fly through the night—a rainbow through the storm—all that exists in nature most aerial, bright and beautiful; these Charles compared her to, and a great deal more; that is—when they first met. Charles, with his great Saxon heart, fell in love with her at first sight. It was not love such as he had felt for Isabel. It struck him like a swift disease. It was not the quiet, settled, brother-like affection which had left him nothing to regret and little to desire; but it was a wild, fierce fever, that preyed on his heart and consumed his life. He would fly; he would escape; he was engaged to Isabel. It must be that she did not love him, else she never could have suffered him to leave her; yet he was bound to her. Honour was not to be lightly sacrificed. Would Pauline, with her large passionate eyes, have given up her lover so coldly? Still he was engaged, and it was a sin and a crime to think of another. He would fly from the danger while he could; he would fight the battle while he had strength. He was resolved, adamant. One more interview with Pauline—but Pauline presented herself accidentally in the midst of these indomitable projects. One glance from her deep sapphire eyes put all his resolutions to flight—duty, like a pale ghost, passing slowly by in the shade.

When fully awake to the truth of his position, Houghton wrote to Isabel. He wrote to her like a madman, imploring her to come out to him immediately; to lay aside all foolish scruples, to think of him only as her husband, to trust to him implicitly, and to save him from destruction. He wrote to her with a fierce emphasis of despair and entreaty that burned like fire in his words.

This letter found Isabel enfeebled by long attendance on her mother; unable to make much exertion of mind or body, and requiring entire repose. That she should be restored to her lover; that she should be happy as his wife, was, for a moment, like a new spring-tide in her life to dream. Then she remembered her father, her dear, patient, noble, self-denying father, to whom she was now everything in life; and she wrote and told Charles that she could not go out to him; but reminded him that his term of absence had nearly expired; and that, when he returned, they should be married, never to be parted again. Why should they not be married in England rather than in Jamaica?

"Thank God I am free!" Houghton exclaimed, when he had read the letter. It dropped from his nerveless hand. He ordered his horse, and rode through the burning tropical sun to Pauline Gerard. Not two hours after the receipt of Isabel's letter he was the accepted lover of the young French heiress.

Poor Isabel! at that instant she was praying for him in her own chamber.

News came to England in due time. Charles himself wrote to Isabel, gently and kindly enough; but unmistakeably. It stood in plain, distinct words, " I am to be married to Pauline Gerard;" and no sophistry could soften the announcement. He tried to soothe her wounded feelings by dealing delicately with her pride. He had been, he urged, only secondary in her heart. She placed others before him, and would make no sacrifice for him. What had happened was her own doing entirely; she had not cared to retain him, and he had only acted as she would have him act, he was sure of that, in releasing her. And then he was " hers very affectionately," and " would be always her friend."

Isabel did not die. She did not even marry another man out of spite, as many women have done. She looked ill; but was always cheerful when she spoke, and declared that she was quite well. She was more than ever tender and attentive to her father; and she went out much less amongst even the quiet society of their quiet home; but she read a great deal, and without effort or pretension she lived over her sweet poem of patience and duty and womanly love.

THE MOTHER'S PRAYER.

Nestling in his mother's breast
  Lay a sleeping child,
Like a wood-dove in its nest,
  Pure and undefiled:
Quiet tears the mother wept,
While her infant sweetly slept.

Softly prayed the mother then,
  From an o'er-full heart,
That—when in the ways of men
  He must bear a part,—
God would teach him to endure,
God would make him strong and pure.

"Father! if it is Thy will
  That his path be rough,
Guide him with Thy spirit still—
  That shall be enough:
In life's darkness—be his sun,
Oh! thou true and Holy One.

Not the victor's wreath or crown
  Ask I for my child,
But Thy smile when strife is done,
  Beaming pure and mild;
And that smile shall brighter seem,
For his troubled earthly dream.

"Not for talents, power, or fame
  Shall my prayer be,
But that through the cross or shame,
  He may trust in Thee;
Leaning gently on Thy arm,
Through the sunshine, through the storm.

"Well I know my faith is dim,
 And my heart is weak;
And in earnest prayer for him
 Oft I dare to speak
Earth-born hopes of peace and rest,
Deeming that my will is best.

"If such wishes ever press
 To my faltering tongue,
If from me in feebleness
 Such a prayer be wrung;
Father—check my wayward will,
Whisper softly—' Peace—be still'—

"Ask I not that every sting
 From his path depart,
But through all the suffering
 Keep him 'pure in heart;'
Then though troubled and distressed,
He shall know Thy will is best."

Brightly o'er the mother's cheek
 Burned a living joy,
While she asked, with soul so meek,
 Blessings for her boy;
And her prayer sweet peace did bring,
Even in the offering.

MRS. HALE'S TWO VISITS.

"GET up from that chair, I want to sit in it!" cried Willie Gordon, a little boy six years old; at the same time pulling at the dress of the lady who was seated in the chair he wished to have.

"Willie, my love, you must not speak in that way. Go and play with your little horse and carriage, there's a dear boy," said Mrs. Gordon, in a coaxing tone. But Willie was not to be coaxed.

"I don't want to play," he replied; "I want to sit in the rocking-chair—I will have it, I will!" and with renewed vigour he pulled at the lady's dress.

"Indeed, Willie, I feel quite ashamed of you," said his mother, in a languid tone.

Mrs. Hale, perceiving that Willie's conduct would receive no check from his mother, and that her barege dress would be the sufferer, if the child's attack on it was prolonged, rose from the rocking-chair, and took another seat.

Willie climbed into the chair with a cry of exultation, and commenced rocking to and fro, violently.

Mrs. Gordon coloured slightly, and said to her visiter,

"I fear, Mrs. Hale, you will think my Willie a bad boy. I own I spoil him a little. But he is my only child: he knows he is mother's pet, and he takes advantage of it sometimes."

"Not a little spoiled; not a *little*," thought Mrs. Hale; but she was too sensible a woman to utter, in the child's presence, anything that might imply blame of his mother. She merely bowed in reply to Mrs. Gordon's half-apology, and began talking on other subjects.

Presently a smart blow on her arm caused Mrs. Hale to look round. Willie had slipped off the rocking-chair, and was standing behind her; and as she turned suddenly, she received another blow from the whip, in her face.

"Willie, Willie!" cried his mother, now seriously concerned; "give me that whip, there's a darling. And go, ask Jane to give you a nice piece of pound-cake."

"I don't care for pound-cake; I want *her*" (pointing to Mrs. Hale) "to be my horse."

"Mother will be your horse, by-and-bye. Now go to Jane. She has something nice for you, I know," rejoined the mother.

"I won't go. I want to stay here," stoutly responded the son.

Meanwhile Mrs. Hale had risen from her seat, for she foresaw who would be the victor in this contest. She had intended to spend the afternoon with her friend, but now she heartily wished to escape from the house where this little tyrant ruled. So, when Mrs. Gordon pressed her to resume her seat, and lay off her bonnet, she declined, saying, she had other calls to make.

Mrs. Gordon accompanied her friend to the door, saying, "I am very sorry Willie behaved so badly. I am afraid his conduct is driving you away. But he is my only child. I cannot bear to thwart him, or to punish him. If I had half-a-dozen children it would be different. I should then form a system of government, and oblige the children to conform to it, and obey me. But where there is only one child, a mother cannot be always scolding; for my part, I can only love and pet my little Willie."

The two ladies shook hands, and parted. Mrs. Hale walked musingly down the street. "Mrs. Gordon gave me a strange excuse for spoiling her child. Easier to govern six than one! But she is not the first mother I have heard say so. Can there be any truth in it? I owe Mrs. Johnson a call; that will give me an opportunity of comparing. Her system of government may be complete, for she has seven or eight children."

A walk of a few minutes brought her to Mrs. Johnson's door. She rang, and after waiting a considerable time, pulled the bell-handle again, when an untidy-looking maid-servant appeared, and in answer to her inquiry, replied that Mrs. Johnson was at home.

"I'm afeard I kept you waiting," said the girl, as she opened the shutters. "Master Tom, for mischeeve, tied up the tongue of the bell. By good chance I seed it trembling like, or yees might have been kept waiting till the gloaming, and I none the wiser."

"There must be some flaw in the system of government," thought Mrs. Hale. A glance round the parlour confirmed her in this opinion. It was in a state of unutterable disorder. Not a single chair was in its place. Three or four were tied together with twine to form "coach and horses." A quantity of loose music was scattered over the floor, and the sofa was occupied by two dolls, and the various articles of their wardrobe.

Mrs. Johnson entered, with a smile of welcome. But the cordiality of her greeting was sadly marred by the look of vexation which overspread her features as she glanced round the room.

"I am very glad to see you, my dear Mrs. Hale. The children have been in here again, I declare! It is an age since I have seen you. Not half an hour ago I set everything to rights. Do take a seat on the sofa," sweeping with her hand the dolls and their dresses into one corner. Then, throwing herself into the rocking-chair, she exclaimed,

"Oh, Mrs. Hale, you, who have no children of your own, can't imagine all a mother has to put up with. I suppose it looks dreadful to you to see the parlour in this state. It is bad enough, to be sure, but what can be expected when there are seven children in the house?"

At this moment the door was burst open, and two little girls rushed in. They paused a moment at sight of the visiter. But it was only for a moment. Running up to the sofa, they commenced exclaiming, and crying, when they found that their dolls had been pushed into a corner.

"Who crushed my doll's bonnet?" cried Julia.

"Look, how this white frock is tumbled!" exclaimed Mary.

"I wish folks would leave my things alone!" rejoined Julia, stamping her foot passionately.

"Don't you see the lady, children?" exclaimed their mother. "I am really quite ashamed of you. Take your dolls away, and go up stairs."

The little girls were silent, but they began arranging their dolls' clothes, wholly unmindful of their mother's command.

Mrs. Johnson, however, did not appear to notice their disobedience. She did not repeat her own injunction, but continued conversing with Mrs. Hale on the troubles of housekeeping, the idleness of her servants, &c. Presently a dispute arose between the little girls. Sharp words were spoken, and Julia struck Mary in the face;

she ran to her mother, who again interposed her weak and disregarded authority.

"Julia, you are a very naughty girl—go up stairs, this instant." Then, taking Mary on her lap, she said, "There, my darling, let mother kiss it, and it will soon be well."

Mary turned away, pettishly, from her mother's proffered kiss, and Julia, having retreated to the other end of the room, began building a doll's house with books, which she took off the centre-table.

Mrs. Johnson sighed, and exclaimed,

"I have no peace or comfort with these children! My health is so indifferent that I cannot exert myself, and they take advantage of my indulgence towards them."

The door opened, and a boy of twelve or thirteen called out,

"Here, girls, come quick; there are soldiers passing."

The little girls ran out of the room, and Mrs. Hale took advantage of their absence to say,

"If you were rather more firm, my dear friend, in requiring obedience *now*, I think you would have less trouble in the end."

"Ah, it is too late, now," said Mrs. Johnson, with a sigh. "If I had begun so with Emma, my eldest child, it would have been well for me. And not only for *me*, but for her, and for all the rest of them. An old aunt gave me good advice, then, but I foolishly disregarded it. I well remember her words: 'Now, Mary, you have but one child, and can devote all your attention to her. Train her *from the beginning* in habits of obedience.

Such training will be a priceless blessing to her through out the whole of her life. And if God grants you more children, you will find that they will be likely to imitate the example of their oldest sister, whether it be for good or for evil. Take my advice, therefore, and train your first-born in habits of obedience.' She spoke truly and wisely, but I was a young and foolish mother. The words 'obedience' and 'authority' sounded harshly to me. I indulged Emma exceedingly, and gave way to her continually. And, oh, how many a heart-ache does she cost me!"

Mrs. Johnson paused, and covered her face with her handkerchief. Mrs. Hale took her hand, and began, soothingly,

"Dearest friend—"

"Do not attempt to console me, my friend, or to palliate my fault. It has been great, and bitter is its punishment. As one after another were added to our little flock, the duties of family government became more and more difficult. My health is feeble, and my time much occupied; my husband is away all day. The only way to keep the children from being entirely ruined, will be to send them all to boarding-school. The two eldest boys are there already. James is to go next month. And I am endeavouring to make up my mind to send away Emma, Mary, and Julia. It is hard thus to part from my children, but I know I have brought this trial on myself by my foolish, false indulgence. My little Lizzie is only three years old—I will try to be firm with her, and train her up in habits of obedience. God grant she may be a comfort to me, and that I may have grace to carry out my resolution!"

In this earnest desire Mrs. Hale cordially joined, and warmly pressing her friend's hand, she took her leave, pondering on her two visits.

MANAGEMENT OF CHILDREN.

CHILDREN are naturally selfish as regards their physical and animal wants; but they are not naturally ungenerous; this may seem a paradox—yet it is true; their feelings are easily touched; their affection for each other is fond and sincere; they will clutch at an apple or a cake, to have the *first* mouthful, but they will readily offer the second to their playfellow, and sympathize in the pleasure with which he eats it. Daily experience proves this; place a child in the corner by way of punishment; for the first five minutes his little brothers and sisters look on with silent awe: then they watch till the teacher's brow is again smooth—then the eldest assumes courage, and exclaims "Mamma, Ellen is good now," and finally all join in chorus, and entreat that she may come out, for they are "sure she will be good," naturally adopting the old Saxon principle of being sponsors for each other's behaviour. The celebrated apothegm, that man rejoices in the misfortunes of his neighbours, does not hold good in children.

But this is a principle diametrically opposed to tole-

bearing, and it is because we believe it to be almost an instinctive principle in children, that we consider it easy to impress on their minds the criminality of that ill nature, on which tale-bearing is founded. In tale-bearing there is mingled malice, dishonesty, and meanness. It springs from all the baser elements of human nature. We are fully sensible of this in adults: although we are too apt to listen with the attention of curiosity to the scandal which Mrs. Jones or Mr. Smith may tell us of their neighbours, we are conscious that in our hearts we not only discredit, but despise them, as the propagators of it. Neither the wealth of Crœsus, nor the beauty of Venus, nor the fascination of Circe, would obtain a husband for the woman who habitually indulged in uncharitable tales of her friends.

A similar antipathy prevails among children towards any of their playmates given to this unhappy vice; and while we admit that it requires much tact and delicacy to correct the failings of one child, by reference to those of another, we think that in this case, there is scarcely any more effective lesson than that which may be drawn from the acknowledged odium which such offenders bring on themselves. But where instances are not at hand to furnish such a lesson, then the proper check is limited to a decided repulse, given in a tone of indignation. Refuse to hear another word, after enough has been said to show the nature of the intended communication; repel the tale-bearer with decision and disgust. To this must be added explanation of the dishonour and ill-nature of all uncalled-for scouting into the sayings and doings of those around us. "How would you like it, if Caroline came to me to tell me of all the foolish things *you* had been saying? What would you think of your brother, if he had been watching *you* when you were cutting up your pinafore, and asked me to whip you for it? or when you snatched away your sister's doll, and put it on the fire?"

The disposition to speak kindly, to think favourably, to act charitably, in respect of others, cannot be too much or too early cultivated in human nature, ere it becomes necessary to teach distinctions between the reality and the semblance of virtue in those around us.

Those who have lived much in the world, never fail to observe the kind feeling that obtains towards men who habitually seek out the good points in a neighbour's character or conduct. No doubt that, in many instances, this lenient bearing proceeds from timidity; in many others, from a servile and mean anxiety to court the reciprocity of good nature—"screen my offences, and I will publish your merits"—in some cases from a natural and cherished dullness of perception to the nature of vicious habits—a sort of " well, after all, I see no great harm in that." This blinking of vice, is not what we mean by charity; but we intend by the term, a disposition to place a favourable construction upon acts admitting either of censure or applause—an inclination to attribute right motives, where such as are wrong are not unequivocally betrayed—a willingness to think the best, where circumstances are ambiguous—and even where Christian principle is obliged to condemn, to find scope for Christian charity, in favourable contrast of that which is occasionally wrong with that which is habitually right. This is a liberality of mind strictly in accordance with the apostolic definition of charity, that "thinketh no evil," and not less so with a manly and generous disposition, that will nevertheless "call a spade, *a spade*," when duty makes it proper to speak out. Such is the disposition we would foster in earliest infancy.

Yet even here, again, discrimination is required; the child must be taught to overlook a brother's or a sister's failings, but not to connive at their faults. And how is this to be done, where the line of demarcation between faults and failings is, in reference to their tender age, necessarily fine? It is not difficult: very little attention will suffice to show whether a complaint of another springs from ill-natured officiousness, or from conscientious duty to the parent. In the one case it is tendered secretly, stealthily—with an "only think, mamma, what Louisa has been doing!" in the other case it is made openly—gravely—bringing up the culprit in hand to listen to the accusation—"Mamma, Louisa has told a story;" the tone and the features alike betray sorrow and concern; and the reporter of the offence shows that she takes no pleasure in making it known, though she dare not conceal it. Here attention must be given, and the accuser and accused both heard with calmness and gravity; and punishment inflicted or withheld, as justice may require.

This doctrine is only applicable to the internal economy of the nursery itself; for in no case ought complaint, however just, or information, however accurate, to be received from a child, as to the proceedings of the parlour or the kitchen. It must indeed be a most mismanaged household, where the children are, even by accident, accessible to knowledge of the misdeeds of either parents or servants. Such knowledge snould find no possibility of access to their ears. We may advert to this hereafter; we content ourselves at present with the observation that, if, with respect to each other, the inmates of the nursery can only be properly permitted to disclose offences in some very special cases, it is scarcely possible to conceive a case, in any well-regulated establishment, where a child can be a proper channel to convey to a parent's ear the indecorums of the household; the door of the nursery or schoolroom should be hermetically sealed to all unsummoned approach.

Lying, sullenness, and tale-bearing, are three of the cardinal points of juvenile delinquency: many would add quarrelling as the fourth, while others would assign equal rank to disobedience. We are inclined, however, to regard both in a more venial light, unless quarrelling is followed up with vindictiveness, or disobedience is persisted in to contumacy. In either of these extreme cases, the fault becomes a crime, and the same duty of insisting on its sinfulness, arises; but simple dissension, caused by a transient impulse of anger, is not matter for stern rebuke; it rather calls for conciliation and expostulation. Children may be induced to check the expression of anger, but will not conquer it merely because they are punished for giving way to it; on the contrary, the very remembrance that they have undergone punishment on a brother's account, often gives a permatuency to angry feeling, which would have evaporated with the moment, had a reconciliation been instantly promoted. It is also proverbially the case, that there is always fault on both sides, and unless the origin of the dispute is actually witnessed, it is most difficult to decide to whom the greater share belongs; hence, if only one is punished, injustice *may* be done; if both undergo the penalty, injustice *must* be done. Yet when cooler feelings return, and they are again susceptible of instruction, too much pains cannot be taken to make the reconciliation perfect, by appealing to their natural affection for each other, and then the weight of the admonition should fall on the elder, even if he happens not to be the aggressor.

Nor is disobedience to be visited with extreme severity; we began with stating it to be a prevailing error in nursery education, to make passive obedience the basis of all discipline; an obedient and a docile spirit is assuredly indispensable to all improvement. But though the rod may make the spirit obedient, it will not make it docile, and the docility is at least as important as the obedience; to obtain both, the reason must be appealed to, and where this appeal is judiciously and habitually made, it will seldom be found that the disobedience of a child amounts to contumacy. When it does, it *must* be subdued: but where it stops short of this, it springs only from thoughtlessness or forgetfulness: and these are not faults to demand more than gentle reproof. We place them only in the same class with untidyness, carelessness, negligence, or impatience.

THE BRIGHT SIDE.

> " Some murmur when their sky is clear,
> And wholly bright to view,
> If one small speck of dark appear
> In their great heaven of blue;
> And some with thankful love are filled
> If but one streak of light—
> One ray of God's great mercy—gild
> The darkness of their night"   TRENCH.

WITH how much force did these lines come to me, as I listened this morning to the petulant complaints of a neighbour, who came in to sit an hour with me! The poor woman would have me believe that her sky was ever cloudy, nor was ever gilded by "one streak of light." Yet she is blessed with an indulgent husband, who loves her as much as he *can* love an habitual grumbler. Her children are active little beings, for whom she ought to feel the deepest thankfulness. The appointments of her household betoken an abundance and the best of this world's goods. She has keen intellect, and the means for satisfying every mental craving; but, alas! her wit is only expended in sarcasm, and in contempt of all that surround her—yes, even of husband, children, and home!

The fiend of discontent sits for ever by her side, and paints all things in dark, distorted lines, and false colouring, and shuts out from her soul's vision the fair, sunny side of life. The "inner eye" recognises nothing of the sweet look which nature wears, nor reflects the shining glory of the material world, nor the tender kindness of human faces. She sees deceit in smiles, treachery in kisses, and guilt in the blush of youth and animation. Her heart is thrilled by no true, sweet echoes. The warbling of woodbirds—the music of waterfalls, and even the gentle speech of friends, have each for her some peculiar monotony, or harshness, or dissonance. Alas! that she should hear little children call her by the sweet, sacred name of *mother*, and not be stirred by holy, softening emotions! They call her mother, but know nothing of maternal advice and sympathy—so precious, so all-healing! Those little children hide from her, most carefully, their faults and sorrows, for they shrink from the sharp invective, the stern, unloving reproof with which their confessions would be received. She has no "bright side" for their griefs, nor tender prayer, nor consoling counsel, for winning the erring one to repentance and hopeful resolves.

Poor things!—there are *step-children* far happier than they, obliged to speak of this sad *mockery* as their *real mother!* Ah! the brother-baby that was taken away by the angels has found, we may believe, his real mother, with her bright face, and her voice soft and musical with affection.

Nor do the children "tell mother" their little pleasures and plans—*that* would be most ruinous policy! She would be sure to discover in every loved amusement some hidden danger, or certain disaster, or dire wickedness, which they, by themselves, would never have found out; and so they prefer, by keeping silence, *never to find it out.*

Little Willie had been told, by his cousins, a long, wonderful, yet "real, true" story of all the delightful things to be enjoyed "out at grandfather's"—of clover fields, haymaking, meadow-larks, poneys, bee-hives, cows, frisky pigs,—and "*such* a dog that knew *everything*"—and "*such* a great, high tree, that can be climbed as easy as a stairway. and from the top of which you can see *almost* to the city!" Then there is an old mysterious garret for rainy days—just like the one Ik Marvel tells about—and *grandmother!*—"she looks exactly like Dame Bountiful in the Fairy Book!" Oh, how the little boy's fancy revelled in these enchanting scenes, and straightway came the daring thought that *he*, Willie, might go and see that good old grandmother, and be a partaker in these darling country sports! At last hope made him bold to face his mother with the request to "go home with grandfather the next time he comes to town."

Oh, what a damper of an answer he got! How sadly the boy's anticipations drooped beneath it! Hear her: "*No*, child, it isn't worth while for you to go out to that dull place for the risk of getting your neck broken, or being drowned in the great pond! Don't say another word about it, but go, now, and study your multiplication-table!" And then in a croaking, soliloquizing tone, "They are certainly the most ungrateful children that ever were born—to *think* of the very youngest fretting to leave his mother's wing!" *Wing*, indeed! To poor Willie it was only a great spectral thing, after the raven or bat order, which was for ever spread between him and all that the wide world had of freedom or delight, and which always came flapping along to brush away his grand, boyish projects, just as they had reached their prime! What a discouraging, dismal mother! To her, gay, light-hearted girls are frivolous, and *all* boys noisy savages, who are, as a matter of course, to be snubbed, and stinted, and *put down!*

Let us leave such a very dark side of the picture, and turn to the cheerful, ever-youthful mother, whose countenance is beaming with love glances and caressing smiles; whose heart is ever ready with its hearty, warm, abundant sympathy; whose very presence brings a sense of safety and comfort. She is so "full of fun," as the little ones say; so inventive, *appreciating*—no one within her sphere grows stupid, morose, or idle. What child, with such a mother, could be naughty for a very long time? *Who* could deceive her?

Her daily life preaches a beautiful, convincing sermon of "good-will towards men." Her patience and self-sacrifice have silent, irresistible force, and the children must needs "do as mother does." Her trust in Divine Providence is so real and practical—her belief in the Bible so firm and loving—her religion so active—and her conscience so delicate—cognisant of the minutiæ of thought, feeling, and deed, that her children catch the inspiration, and learn to *love* to "do as mother does." Manhood and womanhood find them ready for all that life has for them to do, strong in the hope, and trust, and belief in which "mother" did rest and live.

READER, have *you* such a mother? Do you help to make that "bright side" to which her eye is ever turned?

I did not think, when I began, of saying so much

FULL OF FUN.

about maternal influence, but my thoughts have ever such tendency.

Every subject is likely to lead me into speculation as to its connexion with the mother and children.

We are all, in every position of life, concerned in this seeking for whatever is beautiful and genial in life. The "Bright Side" is the side of truth and goodness, in whatever forms they may be manifested. It is bounded by no conditions, high or lowly, nor seasons, nor climes, nor age. It belongs to that world in which every pure, affectionate spirit does live, and encloses that unfading garden of Paradise which such a spirit makes for itself. It takes its light from Heaven. Neither poverty, nor hard labour, nor pain, nor separation from friends, can darken that spiritual radiance.

DEAR READERS—let us not only look with "thankful love" on every ray which God's great mercy sends us, but let us seek continually in all people the kind, the true, and the amiable. For there is no human being, however degraded, that possesses not some spark of goodness, and some divine truth which that spark keeps alive.

Let us meet the stranger without suspicion, or desire to know his faults. Let us be our own judge of him, closing our hearts against all that gossip or slander may say. We will meet him with the " charity that *hopeth* all things." We will receive him as the angels receive a new comer from this world—eager to discover what he has that is wise and good, and to cherish and encourage in him all heavenly affections.

And now let me leave you with an appropriate couplet

from the author whose verses I quoted in opening this appeal for the Bright Side:—

> "Envy detects the spots in the great orb of light,
> And Love, the little stars in the darkest, saddest night."

A WORD TO PARENTS.

LET the parent take care to keep humility ahead of self-confidence. Let him cherish the hope in the child of becoming something worthy, amiable, and intelligent *in future*, rather than the thought of his being such already. Let him practically impress the child, that the attainments which the wisest have made, as compared with those which are yet to be acquired, are as a drop of water compared to the whole ocean! Let him remember the Lord's caution to us against self-esteem and self-merit, where he says, "When ye shall have done *all those things* which are commanded you, say, We are unprofitable servants: we have done *only* that which was our duty to do." This passage, in other words, may read thus:—"We have yielded that only which we could not withhold without robbery; we have paid but a very small part of an old debt; and far be the thought from us, that we can bring our Maker into debt to us, or to our merit!" And, remembering this complete antidote to self-gratulation, should not a wise parent, by some sentiment analogous to it, endeavour to counteract the intoxicating quality of praise? How careful we are, supposing we are administering ardent spirit to a child under bodily ailment, lest, by giving too much, we should injuriously inflame! It would be well if a caution which appears to correspond to this, were as carefully observed; that is, a caution lest praise should do hurt, by inflaming the self-love through its injudicious or immoderate application.

Might not a parent say beneficially to a child something to the following effect? "My dear child! You have done well; you have done your duty; I commend you; and rejoice while I compare your attainments with your age and capability; I praise your diligence and care; I present you with a reward as a testimony of my love and approbation; but I should leave my duty unfulfilled if I did not remind you, that the benefit of your improvement and well-doing is entirely your own; that no one can owe you anything because you have done well; but, on the contrary, you yourself are become a debtor to your Heavenly Father for the disposition and ability which he has given you to become good and wise, for goodness and wisdom are his best gifts, being the only springs of true happiness. While, then, I praise you, or whenever any one else praises you, it becomes you to take such praise only as a testimony, that you owe to your Heavenly Father still higher praise, for giving you a title to receive praise from me, or from others; and then you will be willing to refer all merit and praise to Him alone. Remember, also, that if I praise you for learning, or doing right, my praise implies that you should refer it back to me, in part, because where would have been your title to such praise, had not I first imparted to you information, and made you sensible of the great privilege and happiness of doing right? You will not then, my dear child, think highly of yourself because I or others praise you, but you will reverence and adore the Lord, who has, in his goodness, given you a good will and ability; and you will esteem and love your parents, because they, by that wise instruction which the Lord has helped them to administer, have opened and directed your faculties to their destined improvement in goodness and knowledge." Thus will the parent teach his child to love his parents more than himself, and to value them more than he values himself; and this will be the best preparation for the child's coming, at maturity, into that regenerate state in which he will love the Lord for his goodness more than himself; (knowing that, of himself he is nothing!) and esteem the Lord's wisdom, that is, THE TRUTH, above his own intellectual powers, attainments, or opinions.

In supposing a child to merit reward and praise from his parents, we are, of course, supposing him to be tractable and teachable. Now the giving such a stimulus as reward and praise is often resorted to as a means of encouraging and cherishing an obedient and teachable disposition; but may not a *bad*, selfish motive be thus inspired, which will do more harm, than the good conduct will do good; and which, *in the end*, by feeding selfishness and self-will, may render a child more untractable and unteachable than ever?

There is a far better way than this of encouraging teachableness; that is, by implanting in the child's mind that very disposition which is the solid ground of it. And here let us recur to the Lord's example, where he says, "If any man will do his will, he shall know of the doctrine whether it be of God." It is here declared, that the capability of learning and being taught the truth, depends upon the willingness to obey the teacher's will, in which there must be a confidence, that such will *is good in its requirements*, and, therefore, that it is good to yield it. By analogy it follows: that the most effectual way to lead a child to learn and imbibe truth is, to beget in him a willingness to obey the parent's will; so that we are again led to the burden of all our arguments, that so far as a child's ill propensities are effectually counteracted, so far the parent's will becomes the child's will; and for the purposes of instruction, the parent's understanding becomes the child's understanding; and, as a consequence, the pure happiness of the regenerate parent becomes, in a degree, the child's happiness; and, as a further consequence, the religion of the parent, the cause of the child's happiness as well as of the parent's, becomes immovably implanted in the child's mind.

HOUSEHOLD MUSIC.

ONE evening, taking my little boy, a child of two and a half years, in my arms, to lull him to rest, as have fond mothers since the world began, I took up a book of simple nursery rhymes, that some one had left on my table, containing the words and music on opposite pages. As I listlessly turned the leaves, and carelessly hummed the music, I heard a soft sigh from my child; but, without apparently noticing him, I sang on, when dewy tears welled out from beneath his closed eyelids; but still I sang, till, nestling closer to my bosom, the little fellow half whispered, his voice broken by sobs, "Oh, mamma, *don't* sing that!" Surprised at the circumstance, I sought for the cause. Examining the book, I found I had been humming the well-known air by Sir J. Stevenson, the Vesper Hymn. I knew no association connected with the air that could awaken such emotion in my boy; the words were entirely common-place, and could not have been the cause; and to determine that question, many weeks after, under like circumstances, I again sang the same air to words totally different, but the same result followed,—first the silent tear, then a burst of mournful weeping.

Often, when I've heard the power of music denied or ridiculed, have I thought of this incident. Tell us, ye wise utilitarians! dwells there not a potent spell in an art that can work effects like these? Tell us, ye learned metaphysicians! what subtler chords vibrate in the human heart, than answer to its touch? Oh, ye mothers! sisters! prize your lovely gift, and by it weave strong bands, wreathe golden chains, binding in one loving circle the dwellers at your hearth-stone.

Oh, ye parents! ye who bend daily at the altar of devotion, lose not the holy influence of this "most sweet" accompaniment; let with your morning orisons—let with your evening sacrifice ascend the voice of praise to the Highest! "for praise is comely, and it is good to sing praises unto our God!" Yea, with the royal psalmist let us say, "I will sing praises while I have being."

Who does not feel and acknowledge the power of the

human voice? In whose memory—how thickly overpiled it may be, with a long life's gathered incrustations, with the thick layers of a stern life's realities—down, deep down in the heart's recesses,—dwells there not the echo of a mother's lullaby—the remembrance of sweet hymns heard in earliest years? In "visions of the night," in dreams of long-gone times and scenes, they come to us like whispers of distant lutes, like the harmony of soft chords, such as one conceives the angels loved to harp.

Because the influence of music is not measurable by a mathematical scale, is not reducible to a logarithmic expression, too many deem its power a fiction of poets and dreamers; but, parents! surrounded by young, impressible minds, reject so false an estimate, and despise not the moulding power you may exert on plastic hearts, by your tuneful praises of the "Lord of Hosts." Silently and unseen, perhaps, you shall plant a seed that "after many days" shall prove a gentle cord to lure back to paths of peace and virtue, a wayward, erring child, who, though widely straying, shall, in some silent watch, hear the still whisper of a reproving conscience, floating in, as it were, upon his soul's ear, in tones of an old, familiar melody—

"Return, oh wanderer! return,
And seek an injured Father's face."

What a reward! what notes of rapture shall sound from the redeemed, over one so reclaimed!

It needs no great skill in the *science* of music for this office in social worship. Sing the old airs and melodies your grandsires sang. The older, simpler, perhaps the dearer. They have the charm of associations of your early days. They are linked with sweet memories of those, perhaps, who have long sung nobler songs, long struck golden lyres. There's no melody on earth so perfect as the blending of kindred voices. Gather, then, your households, and attune their hearts and voices to sing "the song of Moses and the Lamb." What medium more fitting by which to celebrate the praises of a Saviour such as ours—to extol a love so ineffable as His? Daily let our voices "beat the heavenward flame," preparing us to join the seraph-choir, if at last we be permitted to

> Soar and touch the heavenly strings,
> And vie with Gabriel while he sings
> In notes that are divine."

LOVE'S YEARNING.

"ARE they all here?"

"Yes, all but one; and she has just waked up from a nap—she will be down soon."

"Isn't it a beautiful sight?" exclaimed a fashionably-dressed woman, sinking languidly into a seat, and smoothing the folds of her thick satin.

"Beautiful, but exceedingly sad," replied another, whose lip trembled, and in whose eyes stood unrestrained tears; "the little darlings are motherless."

"Yes, but how well they are provided for! Just look at that sweet little thing with the auburn curls. Isn't she pretty?"

Pretty she was, indeed; nay, beautiful, with her little round limbs full of dimples—the short frock hanging archly over the plump ankles. A sight worth seeing was that band of motherless children. There was one they called Matty, with bright, crisp curls, and dancing eyes —another who answered to the name of Lilly, with eyes as blue as heaven, and brow as fair as unstained snow. Some were plain and sickly, but most had the rosy glow--the smile unconscious, yet happy, of confiding infancy.

"Many years ago," said Mrs. Eastman, turning to the matron, " I promised a dear friend that, in the event of her death, if she left daughters, they should be taken to my heart and home. She was unfortunate after that, I heard—though I lost sight of her—and died miserably poor. I traced her to this city, and here, they tell me, is her only child—a girl.

"The name ?" asked the matron.

" A plain one—Mary Harson; her mother was beautiful," she added, running her eye along the group, and among the sparkling faces and curly heads.

"Bring Mary Harson down," said the matron to an assistant; and Mrs. Eastman, startled from her composure, uttered an exclamation of surprise as the child entered.

She was a little, odd figure, with large eyes, almost preternaturally bright, thin in form, neither elastic in limb nor rosy of cheek. She came forward with painful timidity, and laid that small, shrunken hand in the gloved hand of the lady, holding it there as if it were not a part of herself—but something she was obliged to offer.

"She's a strange child," said the matron, reading the glance of her visiter, "but intelligent. Her great fault is her sensitive temperament; she never ceases mourning for her mother—that for so little a child is singular, you know—and she dead so long."

Mrs. Eastman had fully expected that one of the most beautiful of that little group was the child of her early friend. Much she was disappointed at the diminutive figure and plain features of this little stranger, and her looks showed her regret. She strove to master it, however, as she gazed at the downcast child—the weak frame so eager to shrink out of notice.

"Will you be my little girl?" she said.

The pale under lip quivered, and the diminutive thumb sought shelter in her mouth, while her eyes were cast towards the floor; but she answered not a word.

"Certainly you will like to go with this lady," said the matron, encouragingly; "you will love to live in a fine house, and have plenty of dolly-babies, plenty to eat, and everybody to love you? Say yes to the lady—she is going to be your mother."

That word broke the loosed fountain—a long-drawn, convulsive sigh, that must nearly have broken her little heart, dilated the child's whole figure—then the tears fell fast and copiously, and she sobbed so violently that Mrs. Eastman exclaimed, pettishly,

"Why, what a queer child it is!" at which the little one sobbed harder than ever—and the matron led her from the room.

* * * * * *

"Tiney, my love, be quiet, and get your lesson. Christmas is coming, you know; and you must do your best. Mary, your eyes are constantly wandering; why *will* you not heed what I say? Are you dreaming?"

The little one started, cast a long, mournful look in the face bent above hers, and, with a deep, oldish sigh, gathered her brows, and resolutely applied herself to her book.

The parlour was beautiful, and well supplied with luxuries. The rich red of the coal glow brought out innumerable pictures of rosewood carving, and struck into vivid light the rare pictures on the wall.

Tiney, a girl with bright black eyes, set in a roguish face, held in her hand a little silver pencil, with which, though her mother did not see her, she was making pictures on the margin of her books. She was the child of wealth; any one might have known that, for the garments folding over those polished limbs were of fine and dainty material. A rich necklace of coral, with golden clasps, encircled her neck; and her little shoes, neatly laced, shone in a casing of the brightest kid. The little girl at her side was not a whit the less beautifully attired; but from her brow the innocent joys, and loves, and sweet surprises of childhood seemed permanently banished. Even the rose-light of health looked only dimly through the transparent cheeks, and her large sad eyes always made one think of something mournful. A chubby babe, almost ready for the nursery, lay quietly upon the lounge, drowsily playing with his blocks, and crowing in an undertone.

"How now!"—that voice was all heart—"How long

have you been dumb—all of you? Come, I'm for a game—rouse up—look something like life!" and Mr. Eastman threw his great frame into an easy-chair, holding out his arms for the now wide-awake baby.

"Tiney, do you know your lesson?"

"Yes, mamma," answered the child, hastily concealing the pencil she had made her plaything.

"And you, Mary?"

"No, mamma," timidly replied the more conscientious Mary.

"Then you must not expect to play," said Mrs. Eastman, sharper than was wont. "There, no crying—I'm tired of it."

"Don't be harsh to her," exclaimed Mr. Eastman, softly; "perhaps she isn't well."

"Then, if she isn't well, she may go to bed," added the lady, impatiently; "but I know better, she is well—and she will be well—and she will look like a funeral all the time, notwithstanding all I have done for her. I hate ingratitude."

"Never mind, Molly, you'll try harder to study tomorrow—won't you?" But the child shrieked convulsively, as his kind voice touched her heart, and laying her head low on her hands, sobbed as she had not for many days.

A bitter look crossed Mrs. Eastman's face. Just then a servant came in. "Take Miss Mary to her room—where she can stay till she feels better," she said, sternly; and her husband, who could think of no cause for such strange conduct, silently acquiesced.

"I shall dislike her by-and-bye, I fear," said the

lady, half-communing with herself. "I don't see what it is—she has every comfort. I'm sure poor Mary, her mother, was one of the most amiable beings that ever lived. How little her child takes after her! She is for ever weeping, notwithstanding all I can do. I've loaded her with toys, and anticipated all her wishes, yet she will be sad and miserable. I don't understand it. I'm out of all patience."

Ah! kind mother and gentle friend, you know not that little tender heart! You could not touch its quivering strings but to wake discordant notes. The spirit so sensitive, shrinking if a breath brushed it too harshly, needed at least something akin to a mother's love. It yearned for the good-night kiss; for the arm placed involuntarily about the slight form; for the gentle pressure sometimes given when least expected. This that little sensitive one longed for—in the far dark distance she looked back, remembering how it had been with her.

Tiney and Mary slept in two small, adjoining chambers. Twice, before bedtime, did Mrs. Eastman send up to know if Mary could come to her supper; but the servant returned, saying she was still "in the sulks," she called it—but she did not know. So the babe was laid sweetly in its cradle. Tiney was carefully disrobed before the warm, shining fire—her snowy night-dress put on—and kneeling, with her white hands raised, and clasped in those of her mother—her little body swaying to the measure of her good-night hymn, she happily prepared for slumber.

"O, dear, oh! dear, dear, dear!" sobbed a small

childish voice, "will God please take me home to Heaven?"

Mrs. Eastman paused in absolute astonishment before she entered Mary's room. The door was slightly ajar—the full moon lay lovingly over little Mary, its beams brightening the white objects about the bed, and making her, with her grieved, upturned face, clasped hands, and streaming eyes, seem like an angel sorrowing over some mortal's untimely sin.

"Oh! I am *so* lonely!" sighed the little thing, still talking to her Father in Heaven—"this mother don't love me—I know she don't—she loves her own little girl, for she kisses her a great deal, and she *looks at her happy;* but, oh, dear God, she don't love me like her! Please take me right to Heaven!"

Mrs. Eastman swallowed her emotion; pity swelled at her heart. She remembered how quick the rebuking word sprang forth at any of her faults; how often she called her "lazy little thing," because she turned dreamily away from her book, and how frequently she sent her to her slumbers without one word of praise, while she almost smothered her own child with caresses.

All this while the child was sobbing as she prayed, "Don't let me cry so much, dear God, because they say I'm cross and wicked! Oh, God, *do* let me think of my own dear mamma, without feeling so very bad; and don't let me think what nice times we used to have when little Willy was alive, and mamma used to smile on us so sweetly! Oh, dear good God, if I might only go to Heaven with my dear mother, I never could want to cry again!"

Mrs. Eastman hurried down stairs, and, going by herself, bitterly wept. She saw all her error, and how sorrowful she was making that young life. Drying her tears, after a prayer for guidance, she hastened up stairs. Little Mary had undressed, and with all a woman's precision had laid her clothes carefully aside.

"Mary," said Mrs. Eastman, in a soft voice.

The child looked round, alarmed.

"Mary, shan't I hear your prayers, love?"

Not a word said the child; but with her great eyes wide open, she came slowly towards her foster-mother, and dropped on her knees; nor did she take her wondering glance from that gentle face till she had repeated the last amen.

"Now kiss me, darling!" said Mrs. Eastman, with trembling voice.

There was a pause of a moment. The child caught her breath; then flung her arms passionately about the neck of her mother, kissing her again and again. With a new impulse the foster-mother strained her to her bosom, and so held her, while the hot tears fell like rain down her cheeks.

"And do you think you can love me?" she murmured, disengaging herself from the rapturous embrace.

"Oh, yes, I *do* love you; I love you like my *own* dear mamma; oh, you never were so good to me before!"

"And you will not cry so much, my darling, and make me sad."

"No, I will never cry, for I think my own mamma has come back from Heaven—my *sorry* has all gone. How kind you are, mamma!" and the beautiful head reposed lovingly, and without rebuke, against the heart beating with such new and sweet tenderness: and when Mrs. Eastman again looked down the child was sleeping, with an angelic happiness playing over her serene countenance.

From that time little Mary was like a new creature It was love she yearned for; her tender nature, like the flower for the dew, pined for its sweet nourishment. Never more she wept without cause—never went alone to her Father, and in agony cried, "Dear God, please take me home to Heaven!"

DEAL GENTLY WITH THE TIMID CHILD.

Mrs. Larford said:—"''Supposing this to be all right, the mother will feel herself from the first the depository of its confidence,—a confidence as sacred as any other, though tacit, and about matters which may appear to all but itself and her, infinitely small. Entering by sympathy into its fears, she will incessantly charm them away, till the child becomes open to reason, and even afterwards, for the most terrible fears are those which have nothing to do with reason; the mother will bring it acquainted with every object in the room or house, letting it handle in merry play everything which could look mysterious to its fearful eyes, and rendering it familiar with every household sound.'

"This is a thought worth remembering," said Mrs

ON GRANDPA'S KNEE.

Larford, laying down her book for a moment; "and it reminds me of a circumstance my nurse once told me, relating to a child of hers. The little girl went to visit an aunt, when about ten years of age; and after she was in bed one night, quite alone, she heard the clock give warning of being about to strike. Not having had a clock in her cottage home, and being consequently unaccustomed to the sound, she became dreadfully alarmed, and when unable to bear the terror of being alone any longer, she rushed to the stairs in the dark, fell, and broke her leg. It *is* of importance, therefore, to make children acquainted with the varied sounds they may hear after they are retired for the night. But to proceed:—

" ' Some of my worst fears in infancy were from lights and shadows. The lamp-lighter's torch on a winter's afternoon, as he ran along the street, used to cast a gleam, and the shadows of the window frames on the ceiling, and my blood ran cold at the sight every day, even though I was on my father's knee, or on the rug in the middle of the circle round the fire. Nothing but compulsion could make me enter our drawing-room before breakfast on a summer morning; and if carried there by the maid, I hid my face in a chair, that I might not see what was dancing on the wall. If the sun shone, as it did at that time of day, on the glass-lustres on the mantel-piece, fragments of gay colour were cast on the wall, and as they danced when the glass drops were shaken, I thought they were alive—a sort of imps! But as I never told anybody what I felt, these fears could not be met or charmed away; and I grew up to an age that I will not mention, before I could look steadfastly at prismatic colours dancing on the wall. Suffice that it was long after I had read enough of optics to have taught my child how such colours came there.

"'Many an infant is terrified at the snadow of a perforated night-lamp, with its round spaces of light. Many a child lives in perpetual terror of the eyes of portraits on the walls, or some grotesque shape in the pattern of the paper-hangings. Sometimes the terror is of the clack of the distant loom, or of the clink from the tinman's, or of the rumble of carts under a gateway, or of the creak of a water-wheel, or of the gush of a mill-race. Everything is or may be terrifying to a timid infant, and it is, therefore, a mother's charge to familiarize it gently and playfully with everything that it can possibly notice, making sport with all sights, and inciting it to imitation of all sounds, from the drone of the pretty bee to the awful cry of the old clothes' man, —from the twitter of the sparrows on the roof, to the toll of the distant church-bell.'"

TWO IN HEAVEN.

"You have two children," said I.

"I have four," was the reply; "two on earth, two in heaven."

There spoke the mother! Still hers! only "gone before!" Still remembered, loved, and cherished, by the hearth and at the board; their places not yet filled, even though their successors draw life from the same faithful breast where *their* dying heads were pillowed. "Two in heaven!" Safely housed from storm and tempest; no sickness there, nor drooping head, nor fading eye, nor weary feet. By the green pastures; tended by the Good Shepherd, linger the little lambs of the heavenly fold. "Two in heaven!" Earth less attractive! Eternity nearer! Invisible cords, drawing the maternal soul upwards. "Still small" voices, ever whispering *come!* to the world-weary spirit. "Two in heaven!" Mother of angels, walk softly! Holy eyes watch thy footsteps, cherub forms bend to listen! Keep thy spirit free from earth-taint; so shalt thou "go to them," though "they may not return to thee."

THE MOTHER AND THE SON.

It is a question long since settled by actual facts, that the son, however wayward he may be, will listen to a mother's voice, and call to remembrance her prayers, even long after her voice may be silent in death, and her prayers for him cease. A young minister of the gospel, now an active labourer in the vineyard of the Lord, says: "At twelve years of age I had stood beside the couch of a dying mother, whose voice had often told me of Jesus, and whose prayers had constantly ascended for her first-born. The hand which had led him to the Sabbath School was now motionless. With weeping eyes and a sad heart, the son saw the coffin placed in he grave."

A few years had passed away, when this young man was led to make one honest effort for his soul's salvation. Having given himself to Christ, he adds: "A mother's prayers were answered, though she did not live to witness the conversion of her son."

Edward Payson, the devoted and successful Portland pastor, was a child of many prayers. From the nature of his father's professional duties, his attention to Edward must have been less frequent than his mother's, and partaken in some degree of a more formal character. The recollections of his mother extend from very early childhood to his latest days. He has been heard to say that though she was solicitous that he might be liberally educated and be an accomplished scholar, yet he could distinctly see that her all-absorbing thought respecting him was, that he might be a Christian. To this end she instructed him in early life, and followed up those instructions with fervent prayers. At the early age of three years he was known to call his mother by his bedside to talk with her about God, and his relations to a future world. In a letter to his parents when in college, he writes thus: "To your admonitions and instructions I am indebted for all the moral and religious impressions which are imprinted on my mind, and which I hope will give me reason to bless you through all eternity." There is abundant testimony in the writings of Payson that he attributes his religious feelings, hopes, and usefulness in life, to early parental influences.

Richard Cecil developed, in early life, a marked character. He was decided, daring, and authoritative; even his school-mates yielded implicit obedience to his commands. But there was united with his almost untameable spirit a generous and manly heart. His mother was pious, and did not fail to use the means for his spiritual welfare. He says: "My mother would put things in my way, and I could not get rid of them." When he was six years old, his mother gave him a little book, "Janeway's Token for Children." He says: "I was much affected on reading it. I wept over it. I got into a corner and prayed that I might be as happy as those little children." His early religious impressions wore away as he began to form acquaintances with young men into whose vices and follies he soon fell, and which was the cause of his gradual departure from his mother's admonitions. He began to avow infidel principles at quite an early age, though he afterwards confessed that he did not *half believe them.*

Here was a painful passage in Cecil's early history; and how must that praying mother feel, after all her counsels and prayers, to see the child of her deepest affections a leader in infidel principles? Ah! that mother believed in God—in the efficacy of prayer. She prayed more earnestly for her boy—and he has left a most impressive memorial of a mother's influence in preserving him, under God, from entirely believing a lie. "I was afraid," he says, "to read any author who treated Christianity in a wise and searching manner. Conscience would recall my early instructions and impressions, while my happiness could only consist with their obliteration." At one time he went with one of his associates to see persons caricatured, when in the personage of a woman was represented those persons who talk about religion. "My friend," he says, "laughed heartily; but I could not, for I knew that I had a Christian mother."

At one time when standing by the bedside of a sick mother, he asked her a question: "Are you not afraid to die?" "No, no!" she replied. "Why does not the uncertainity of another state give you no concern?" "She looked me in the face," says Cecil, "with a holy and heavenly smile, which cannot be effaced from my memory, and replied, 'Because God has said to me, Fear not; when thou passest through the waters, I will be with thee.' The remembrance of this scene has oftentimes since drawn an ardent prayer from me that I might die the death of the righteous."

Grace at last conquered the opposition of Cecil's heart to the truth of the gospel. The seed which was faithfully sown by the hand of a Christian mother, and watered with her tears in prayer, though it lay long buried in the heart, at length sprung up, and grew with astonishing vigour, and he stood out in the world a noble champion for God and His truth. Parental influence thus cleaves to the man, and a mother's prayers are heard and answered.

Another striking illustration of a mother's influence is seen in the early history of Philip Doddridge, whose name is ever associated with "The Family Expositor" and the "Rise and Progress of Religion in the Soul." He first saw the light in an obscure street in London, a frail flower then, for he was laid away soon after his birth as dead. He had a mother of earnest prayer and living piety. She taught her children to love the Scriptures, by describing the scenes in the Bible, in a familiar manner, on the old Dutch tiles which lined the chimney corner. Little did the mother of Doddridge anticipate his future career, when he reclined on her knee, followed the direction of her fingers in the Bible, and in childlike simplicity listened to the words of eternal life. When she laid her hand on his head and prayed that he might be a child of God, she did not know that God was preparing him, through her instrumentality, to stand up in the pulpit at Northampton, on Castle Hill, and preach the gospel with so much success.

MOTHER.

YEARS have rolled away since these eyes looked their last, in this world, upon "Mother," yet I cannot now write the name, but it sends a thrill of joy and sorrow through my frame. Joy that I had *such* a mother; sorrow that I was so soon deprived of her priceless counsel and sympathy. While I think of it, ere I am aware, my eyes fill with tears, and those tender chords of affection that bound me to her, vibrate again with all their wonted vigour, and she seems near me still. I hear her voice—I feel her hand upon my head—I see her, as once I did, and rejoice in her presence. But when my senses would realize the fact, I am like the man who has lost an arm; he feels the hand, the fingers as they were, though amputated years ago; but when, with the other, he would touch it, 'tis not there.

Oh, how indelibly does the mother stamp her moral precepts upon the hearts of her children! Has she a tender conscience, venerating the word of God as its *only* guide? You may trust her children, if *she* lived to train them until they became active citizens. 'Tis true sin may hide for years, and seem to annihilate her principles, yet they are "like fire in the bones," as the prophet says, or like a pent volcano in the bosom. Sooner or later they will burn out, and the pastor or Christian teacher finds that the foundation for his work was laid years ago, in the prayers and tears of a FAITHFUL mother; and he, under God, is only permitted to clear away a little of the rubbish, and bring to light what that mother has done. I sometimes think it is well that mothers do not FULLY comprehend the power they possess; if they did they would sink under the weight of their responsibility. Oh, if there be any difference, surely, nearest, and dearest to the Saviour's heart, is the patient, faithful, Christian mother.

Seeing, in a recent publication, an article headed the " Door in the heart," I have endeavoured to embody the sentiment with some additions and alterations in the following lines. Should they encourage any in a persevering labour of love, they will fulfil their desired object.

THE KEY TO THE HEART.

No bandit on the mountain,
 No robber on the plain,
But hath within a fountain
 Of sympathy to gain.

No tyrant o'er a nation,
 Though Nero were his name,
No outcast in creation,
 But hath some sense of shame.

No heart how hard soever,
 And calloused o'er by sin,
But there we may discover
 Some door to enter in.

The way is often winding,
 That hidden door to reach;
Yet sure 'tis worth the finding
 Salvation's truths to teach.

Take with you constant kindness,
 Be sympathy your guide—
Not long you'll grope in blindness,
 The key is on your side.

Nine times in ten, I'll venture,
 A mother's name you'll find
Has been the key to enter
 That door within the mind.

Then bear thy burden, mother,
 Aye bear it patiently,
Thy name is like no other,
 The heart's most sacred key.

"LITTLE THINGS."

A WRITER in the Mother's Journal speaks wisely on the importance of little things:—

Due consideration and strict watchfulness in little things, are of importance to the happiness and welfare of all,—but how especially do little things commend themselves to the attention of a *mother!* In the sphere of her duties can anything be esteemed little or trifling? We think not. She has to deal with little folks. To the mother is intrusted the directing and the moulding of little intellects just beginning to bud and to expand. Can anything be deemed trifling that influences, whether for good or evil, these young but immortal minds? Oh, let a mother weigh well her words, before she allows herself to say of anything pertaining to the little ones around her, "It is but a trifle."

Your little boy utters an untruth. Do not say, "It was about a mere trifle, and besides it did not deceive me for a moment. It is not worth while to make a fuss about it!" A trifle! Is it a trifle in the estimation of that little fellow? It did not deceive you! Did he not *mean* to deceive? Oh, as you value his future happiness and your own peace of mind in after years, beware how you pass lightly over the least departure from truth. Gloss it over with no softening terms. Let the little one of two years old know that a lie is displeasing in the sight of the great God. Let him see and feel that nothing can grieve or displease his mother more than to hear her darling "tell a lie." Speak of it ever with contempt and disgust, and let him see in every word and action the high value you set upon TRUTH.

On entering the breakfast room you perceive a little hand hastily withdrawn from the sugar bowl, or from the plate of biscuit. Do you say, "Well, I'm sure a lump of sugar, or a biscuit is a mere trifle. And the child is heartily welcome to it. I hope you would not pretend to call that stealing." What does the child herself consider it to be? Why was the little hand so hastily withdrawn? Why are her cheeks like crimson, and why is her manner so confused? Does she not know that she has taken what was not her own? Is there not a monitor within which tells her she has done wrong? If you pass by the act as too trifling for your notice, it will be repeated again and again. She also will consider it as a trifle, and the habit, the fearful habit of pilfering will grow upon her. Little by little— little by little; till at last whatever she wishes for, she will take, provided only she thinks herself secure against detection. And what misery will be yours if one day you awaken to the consciousness that your cherished daughter hides, beneath a lovely exterior, the hideous sin of theft, and its twin brother, lying! You start with horror from the very thought. Beware how you pass over the slightest act of pilfering, lest you one day find it to be a dreadful reality.

To turn to less serious matters. You look with pleasure on a well-bred child. You say, perhaps, "I wish my children would keep their clothes neat, and try to give civil answers when a stranger speaks to them." Have you watched them in these respects? Or have you allowed many a little instance of rudeness to pass unreproved? and considered it too troublesome and fussy to teach them habits of cleanliness? Is "Give me some bread;" "I want some pie;" "Get me my hat," the usual way in which your children make known their wants? and do you let them have the things they ask for thus, because you "don't like to make a fuss about such trifles?" No wonder then that they grow up rude and uncouth in speech. It is as easy and pleasant for a child to say, " Please," and " Thank you," *if he is taught from the first to do so*, as it is for him to say, " Give me this," " I want that." It will require, it is true, constant attention to this *little* matter till the habit is formed. But is it not worth the trouble? Rudeness of manner may seem a trifle at two years old. Is it a trifle by the time the boy reaches twelve or fourteen years of age?

We might go on multiplying examples, but the few hints we have already given will suffice. And we wish to add a word or two upon the importance, on the other hand, of noticing and encouraging every little effort to do right.

A mother should endeavour, as far as possible, to enter into her child's thoughts and feelings, and to view things as he views them. Then she will be able in some degree to estimate the greatness of the struggle in the little bosom, as the child stands making up his mind to lend a favourite plaything to his little sister; and the pleasant "Here, Fanny, you may play with my cart till you are tired of it," will not be passed unnoticed, but receive the wished-for kiss of approbation.

The love of praise is stronger in children than at any other period of life. Children may certainly be overpraised, and flattery has sown the germ of much evil in the youthful heart; but we do think that very many err on the opposite extreme. They are busy and do not notice the child's little effort to win an approving smile; or something has put them out of humour, and they do not feel in a mood to praise.

The blocks have all been arranged in their box, and the playthings put neatly away, and the little boy runs to his mother to tell her of his industry. If she merely says, hurriedly, "Very well, very well, now you can go up to bed," what a disappointment she will cause to the little heart that expected a pleasant smile and an approving "There's a good boy."

Such encouragement consumes very little time; it need encroach on none of your duties. But it does make one important demand on you, which is, that your attention be continually alive to everything which may promote the progress and improvement of your child; and that your hearty sympathy be at once aroused by every little effort which he makes towards well doing.

And is this too much to ask of a mother? Is it not your highest duty, your sweetest privilege, to direct, to support and encourage those trembling little steps which without your watchful guidance will surely stray in paths of error and of sin? The steps are feeble and faltering now, the progress is slow; but, Christian mother, let yours be the blessed task of placing those little feet in the right way, and aiding them in their gradual progress, and then yours will be the bright reward of beholding them in later years *running* with patience the race set before them, "pressing on towards the mark for the prize of the high calling of God in Christ Jesus."

Doubt it not, for the word of the Lord has spoken it.

THE CHILDREN AND THE NOVEL.

"WELL there," muttered Mrs. Lee, in a somewhat petulant tone, as she laid down her babe; "thank fortune, as the last one is abed and asleep. Now for a little comfort."

Carefully drawing the blankets around the tiny form, she rested one hand for a few moments upon the gently heaving breast, stirred the cradle with the other, singing the while a low lullaby.

Assured from its soft breathing, and quiet limbs, that it was indeed asleep, she turned from it quickly, drew her low rocker to the stand, picked up the light, and took, from underneath a miscellaneous pile in her work basket, an uncut novel.

"What a beautiful title!" said she, all traces of weariness vanishing with electric rapidity from her countenance. As her eye glanced over its pages, the dull look they had worn all day disappeared, and the light of anticipated joy flashed in its stead.

"I know that I shall be pleased with it. I feel that it will be interesting," continued she.

"What charming names the author has chosen. None of your Johns and Hannahs, your Roberts and Margarets—oh no! here is noble Rodrigo, poetic Clarence, sweet Florilla, saintly Therese: why, there is not an ordinary name in the book. The writer must be one of unusual taste!"

Having hastily cut the leaves, she shaded her brow with one hand, grasped the charming book with the other, as though it were polished gold and she a miser, and commenced, in the phrase of enthusiastic novel readers, to devour the pages.

Rapidly did her eyes run over the first chapter. But then—she turned her head with a quick, impatient movement. Did she not hear a noise in the cradle? Yes, a little hand was lifted from beneath the cover.

"Too bad, too bad; he'll be awake all the evening now;" and she glided with a noiseless step to the child's side.

But the eyelids were still closed; the measured breath of slumber stole gently from the half-parted lips, and the offending hand rested in quiet beauty upon the soft neck.

It was a fair, sweet babe, whose little heart had throbbed but one short summer. As it lay there, the spell of sinless sleep upon its brow, it seemed the type of all things pure and blest. Eden, with all its loveliness, never charmed the gaze of Eve with such a picture. The holier feelings of the mother's breast were touched, as if by a hand from heaven. The angel began to trouble the deep waters of her soul as she stood beside that cradle-bed; and when after a vigil of several moments, the child still sleeping, she bent her head and imprinted upon its lips the kiss of love, the healing wave flowed for an instant, then ebbed, for the novel was not yet read..

Resuming her seat, Mrs. Lee again took her book. But the fiction seemed to have lost some of its fascination. For some time her glance vacillated between its finely printed pages and her heaped-up basket. She even put on her thimble and threaded a needle. But a moonlight scene, where, in a honeysuckle bower, the noble lover draws a trembling girl to his bosom, and pours into her ears the bewitching words of wild courtship, acted like magic on the reader's mind, and she became absorbed in the glowing picture.

The second and third chapters were soon perused, and she was entering with interest upon the fourth, when a sweet voice from the trundle-bed called out, "Mother, mother. mother!"

Her ear caught the sound; but it made no impression upon her mind till it had been several times repeated; then turning quickly, in no very gentle voice, she exclaimed, "What do you want, Lizzie? I thought you were asleep an hour ago."

"I have been asleep, mother," answered the daughter, in a timid tone. "I waked up because"—

"Because you were a naughty girl and wanted to plague me. Strange that I can't have a minute's comfort," and going hastily to the bed, she drew the clothes around the child, and bade her shut her eyes and go to sleep.

"I want a drink, mother; I can't sleep, I am so thirsty."

The mother looked around; there was neither pitcher nor glass in the room.

"It's always just so. I never forget to bring water but you are sure to want some. Why didn't you drink last night, when I had a whole pitcher full for you?"

"I wasn't thirsty last night. Do please give me a drink, and I'll go right to sleep."

"I'm not going to run down stairs to-night; so just turn over and shut your eyes."

And she sat down again to her novel, leaving the thirsty child to its thoughts, or dreams, as the case might be.

Lizzie, as she said, wanted a drink very much, and so she turned and tossed, and tried to think of everything but water, while that was all she could think of.

"If I only had one little swallow," murmured she to herself, "I think I could get along till morning." But she might as well have wanted a pailful; there was no prospect of getting any. By-and-by, she spied upon the stove hearth a tin cup. "The baby's milk!" said she. "Perhaps that would be as good as water. I wonder if mother would let me have it?" She looked toward the parent. She was absorbed in her book; her very being seemed bound up in it. The child knew too much to disturb her.

But perhaps she could get it without disturbing her mother, and she did want a drink so much. She hesitated awhile, then crept silently out of bed, stole to the cup, seized it eagerly, and took a swallow But it tasted better than she thought it would, and her thirst was such that she drained it. Alarmed at what she had done, she was in such haste to put it back that it slipped from her trembling hand, bounding against the stove, falling on the hearth, and rolling thence on the carpet.

"Why, Lizzie Lee!" screamed the mother, dropping her book and running to the child. "I should like to know what you've been about; spilt all the baby's milk, I'll warrant," as she took up the empty cup. Then seeing the carpet was quite dry, she seized Lizzie by the shoulder, exclaiming in an angry voice, "What have you done with the milk, you little plague? Tell me this minute what's become of it?"

"I was so thirsty, mother," answered the child in a pleading voice, tears starting to her eyes, "I could not go to sleep, and so"—

"So you drank it, did you! you naughty girl," continued Mrs. Lee with increased vehemence of tone; "drank it, and I haven't another drop of milk in the house. I'll teach you to do such things;" and her hand came down heavily upon the shrinking shoulder, one! two! three times! A wild scream of pain burst from the child's lips. Another and another, and angry and excited as the mother was, they pierced her heart with deep arrows.

The noise startled another child who slept in the same bed with Lizzie. Frightened from its sound slumbers, it shrieked in alarm, when the babe, waking at the same moment, joined its voice with the others, not in harmony, but in discords which echo so often in the nursery, stunning the ear and bewildering the brain.

With quick steps, quick hands, and a softened tone, Mrs. Lee strove to calm the tempest she had raised. Lizzie's cries soon merged into piteous sobs, but Willie and the babe continued their loud screams, till the mother, in her perplexity, would fain have wrung her hands and sat down and wept with them. She ran from one to the other, soothing, singing, and caressing. But they would not hush in the least, till, as a last resource, she took the baby in one arm, Willie in the other, and, thus burthened, paced the chamber. Her limbs ached with the effort, her voice grew plaintive, her heart sad and sore with the upbraidings of conscience which she had striven too long to stifle. She breathed sweet music in the ears of the little sobbing creatures who struggled in her arms, but not a word of anger escaped from her pale lips. She felt she was the guilty cause of all her trouble. A little forethought, a little self-denial, a little discipline of temper, and all had been well.

It was a long time ere she ventured to sit down and rock the children, and they did not soon close their eyes in sleep. They would start and scream, then draw back such long sighs, that the tears which trembled in the mother's eyes would flood her cheeks.

When, at last, they rested in a sweet, calm slumber, she was at a loss how to put them down to release her weary arms, without the risk of new confusion. There was no one whom she could call upon for aid. No one? Yes, there was the little trembling creature whose tender skin still smarted with the chastisement of an angry mother.

"Lizzie," called the mother, after a long while, in a very low gentle tone.

The child was quickly beside her.

"Bring your little chair, and sit down close to me and see if you can draw the baby on your lap without waking him."

Lizzie did as directed, and the babe was soon clasped to her heart, her lips breathing childish words of affection over its unconscious form.

Very carefully did Mrs. Lee lay down her little Willie, and for some moments she sat beside him smoothing gently his fair brow, twining his golden locks around her fingers, and pressing the softest and sweetest of kisses upon his still lips.

Then going to Lizzie, she took from her arms the sleeping babe, and placing it in the cradle, bent over it, whispering the fondest terms of endearment.

Sitting down beside it, she covered her face, and thought grew busy. By-and-by, Lizzie stole quietly to the chair, knelt beside it, and buried her head in her mother's lap. Mrs. Lee's hands toyed with the soft brown curls that fell over it in such rich profusion, and several times pushed them off the forehead, when the child felt the mute pressure of her lips. For some time both were silent. At length Lizzie looked timidly up, saying, in a touching voice,

"I am *so* sorry, mother, I made you so much trouble. I'll try and never be thirsty again when you are reading."

The mother's heart started; she drew the child to her bosom, embraced it fondly, closely, as though she thought by pressure to still its painful throbbings. Then bearing her to the bed, she set her down and hastily left the room. She soon returned, a glass of water in her hand. "Thank you, mother," said Lizzie, when she had quenched her thirst, "*you will have a good time to read now*, for I shall go right to sleep."

With her eyes brimful of tears, the mother bent over her child and kissed her again and again. And Lizzie, feeling that she was quite forgiven, and not dreaming that she had been more sinned against than sinning, threw her arms around her parent's neck, and gave back kiss for kiss; then nestling on the warm pillow of her little brother, she closed her weary eyes and in a few minutes was sound asleep.

For a long while the mother knelt beside the low couch, and when she rose and sat down again by the stand, she left the novel where she had dropped it, but took from her basket an unfinished doll, and with rapid fingers plied her needle.

It was long ere she placed her head upon her pillow. When she did, the doll, completed and neatly dressed, lay by the side of Lizzie; the novel, half-read, upon the Lehigh in the stove, a handful of light ashes.

A REVELATION OF CHILDHOOD.

Mrs Jameson has given us the following deeply interesting revelation of her childhood. There are lessons in it which every parent should lay to heart. She says:—

We are all interested in this great question of popular education; but I see others much more sanguine than I am. They hope for some immediate good result from all that is thought, written, spoken on the subject day after day. I see such results as possible, probable, but far, far off. All this talk is of systems and methods, institutions, school-houses, schoolmasters, schoolmistresses, school-books; the ways and the means by which we are to instruct, inform, manage, mould, regulate, that which lies in most cases beyond our reach—the spirit sent from God. What do we know of the mystery of child-nature, child-life? What indeed do we know of any life? All life we acknowledge to be an awful mystery, but child-life we treat as if it were no mystery whatever —just so much material placed in our hands to be fashioned to a certain form, according to our will or our prejudices—fitted to certain purposes, according to our notions of expediency. Till we know how to *reverence* childhood we shall do no good. Educators commit the same mistake with regard to childhood that theologians commit with regard to our present earthly existence; thinking of it, treating of it, as of little value or significance in itself, only transient, and preparatory to some condition of being which is to follow—as if it were something separate from us and to be left behind us as the creature casts its skin. But as in the sight of God this life is also something for its own sake, so in the estimation of Christ, childhood was something for its own sake,—something holy and beautiful in itself, and dear to him. He saw it not merely as the germ of something to grow out of it, but as perfect and lovely in itself as the flower which precedes the fruit. We misunderstand childhood, and we misuse it; we delight in it, and we pamper it; we spoil it ingeniously, we neglect it sinfully; at the best we trifle with it as a plaything which we can pull to pieces and put together at pleasure—ignorant, reckless, presumptuous that we are!

And if we are perpetually making the grossest mistakes in the physical practical management of childhood, how much more in regard to what is spiritual! What do we know of that which lies in the minds of children? we know only what we put there. The world of instincts, perceptions, experiences, pleasures, and pains, lying there without self-consciousness,—sometimes helplessly mute, sometimes so imperfectly expressed, that we quite mistake the manifestation—what do we know of all this? How shall we come at the understanding of it? The child lives, and does not contemplate its own life. It can give no account of that inward, busy, perpetual activity of the growing faculties and feelings which it is of so much importance that we should know. To lead children by questionings to think about their own identity, or observe their own feelings, is to teach them to be artificial. To waken self-consciousness before you awaken conscience, is the beginning of incalcu'able mischief. Introspection is always, as a habit, unhealthy: introspection in childhood fatally so. How shall we come at a knowledge of life such as it is when it first gushes from its mysterious fountain head? We cannot reascend the stream. We all, however we may remember the external scenes lived through in our infancy, either do not, or cannot consult that part of our nature which remains indissolubly connected with the inward life of that time. We so forget it that we know not how to deal with the child-nature when it comes under our power. We seldom reason about children from natural laws, or psychological data. Unconsciously we confound our matured experience with our memory: we attribute to children what is not possible, exact from them what is impossible;—ignore many things which the child has neither words to express, nor the will nor the power to manifest. The quickness with which children perceive, the keenness with which they suffer, the tenacity with which they remember, I have never seen fully appreciated. What misery we cause to children, what mischief we do them, by bringing our own minds, habits, artificial prejudices and senile experiences, to bear on their young life, and cramp and overshadow it —it is fearful!

Of all the wrongs and anomalies that afflict our earth, a sinful childhood, a suffering childhood, are among the worst.

O, ye men! who sit in committees, and are called upon to legislate for children,—for children who are the offspring of diseased or degenerate humanity, or the victims of a yet more diseased society,—do you, when you take evidence from jailors, and policemen, and parish schoolmasters, and doctors of divinity, do you ever call up, also, the wise physician, the thoughtful physiologist, the experienced mother? You have accumulated facts, great blue books full of facts, but till you know in what fixed and uniform principles of nature to seek their solution, your facts remain a dead letter.

I say nothing here of teaching, though very few in truth understand that lowest part of our duty to children. Men, it is generally allowed, *teach* better than women, because they have been better taught the things they teach. Women *train* better than men, because of their quick intinctive perceptions and sympathies, and greater tenderness and patience. In schools and in families I would have some things taught by men, and some by women: but we will here put aside the art, the act of teaching: we will turn aside from the droves of children in national schools and reformatory asylums, and turn to the individual child, brought up within the guarded circle of a home or a select school, watched by an intelligent, a conscientious influence. How shall we deal with that spirit which has come out of Nature's hands unless we remember what we were ourselves in the past? What sympathy can we have with that state of being which we regard as immature, so long as we commit the double mistake of sometimes attributing to children motives which could only spring from our adult experience, and sometimes denying to them the same intuitive tempers and feelings which actuate and agitate our maturer life? We do not sufficiently consider that our life is not made up of separate parts, but is *one*—is a progressive whole. When we talk of leaving our childhood behind us, we might as well say that the river flowing onward to the sea had left the fountain behind.

I will here put together some recollections of my own child-life; not because it was in any respect an exceptional or remarkable existence, but for a reason exactly the reverse, because it was like that of many children: at least I have met with many children who throve or suffered from the same or similar unseen causes even under external conditions and management every way dissimilar. Facts, therefore, which can be relied on, may be generally useful as hints towards a theory of conduct. What I shall say here shall be simply the truth so far as it goes; not something between the false and the true, garnished for effect,—not something half-remembered, half-imagined,—but plain, absolute matter of fact.

No; certainly I was not an extraordinary child. I have had something to do with children, and have met with several more remarkable for quickness of talent, and precocity of feeling. If anything in particular, I believe I was particularly naughty,—at least so it was said twenty times a day. But looking back, now, I do not think I was particular even in this respect; I perpetrated not more than the usual amount of mischief—so called—which every lively, active child perpetrates between five and ten years old. I had the usual desire to know, and the usual dislike to learn; the usual love of fairy tales, and hatred of French exercises. But not of what I learned, but of what I did *not* learn; not of what they taught me, but of what they could not teach me; not of what was open, apparent, manageable, but of the under current, the hidden, the unmanaged or unmanageable, I have to speak, and you, my friend, to hear and turn to account, if you will, and how you will. As we grow old, the experiences of infancy come back upon us with a strange vividness. There is a period when the overflowing, tumultuous life of our youth rises up between us and those first years; but as the torrent subsides in its bed, we can look across the impassable gulf to that haunted fairy land which we shall never more approach, and never more forget!

In memory I can go back to a very early age. I perfectly remember being sung to sleep, and can remember even the tune which was sung to me—blessings on the voice that sang it! I was an affectionate, but not, as I now think, a lovable or an attractive child. I did not, like the little Mozart, ask of every one around me, "Do you love me?" The instinctive question was, rather, "Can I love you?" Yet certainly I was not more than six years old when I suffered from the fear of not being loved where I had attached myself, and from the idea that another was preferred before me, such anguish as had nearly killed me. Whether those around me regarded it as a fit of ill-temper, or a fit of illness, I do not know. I could not then have given a name to the pang that fevered me. I knew not the cause, but never forgot the suffering. It left a deeper impression than childish passions usually do; and the recollection was so far salutary, that in after life I guarded myself against the approaches of that hateful, deformed, agonizing thing which men call jealousy, as I would from an attack of cramp or cholera. If such self-knowledge has not saved me from the pain, at least it has saved me from the demoralizing effects of the passion, by a wholesome terror, and even a sort of disgust.

With a good temper there was the capacity of strong, deep, silent resentment, and a vindictive spirit of rather a peculiar kind. I recollect that when one of those set over me inflicted what then appeared a most horrible injury and injustice, the thoughts of vengeance haunted my fancy for months; but it was an inverted sort of vengeance. I imagined the house of my enemy on fire, and rushed through the flames to rescue her. She was drowning, and I leaped into the deep water to draw her forth. She was pining in prison, and I forced bars and bolts to deliver her. If this were magnanimity, it was not the less vengeance; for, observe, I always fancied evil, and shame, and humiliation to my adversary; to myself the *rôle* of superiority and gratified pride. For several years this sort of burning resentment against wrong done to myself and others, though it took no mean or cruel form, was a source of intense, untold suffering. No one was aware of it. I was left to settle it; and my mind righted itself I hardly know how: not certainly by religious influences—they passed over my mind, and did not at the time sink into it,—and as for earthly counsel or comfort, I never had either when most needed. And as it fared with me then, so it has been in after life; so it has been, *must* be, with all those who, in fighting out alone the pitched battle between principle and passion, will accept no intervention between the infinite within them and the infinite above them; so it has been, *must* be, with all strong natures. Will it be said that victory in the struggle brings increase of strength? It may be so with some who survive the contest; but then how many sink! how many are crippled morally for life! how many, strengthened in some particular faculties, suffer in losing the harmony of the character as a whole! This is one of the points in which the matured mind may help the childish nature at strife with itself. It is impossible to say how far this sort of vindictiveness might have penetrated and hardened into the character, if I had been of a timid or retiring nature. It was expelled at last by no outer influences, but by a growing sense of power and self-reliance.

In regard to truth—always such a difficulty in education,—I certainly had, as a child, and like most children, confused ideas about it. I had a more distinct and absolute idea of honour than of truth,—a mistake into which our conventional morality leads those who educate and those who are educated. I knew very well, in a general way, that to tell a lie was *wicked;* to lie for my own profit or pleasure, or to the hurt of others, was, according to my infant code of morals, worse than wicked—it was *dishonourable.* But I had no compunction about telling *fictions;* inventing scenes and circumstances which I related as real, and with a keen sense of triumphant enjoyment in seeing the listener taken in by a most artful and ingenious concatenation of impossibilities. In this respect "Ferdinand Mendez Pinto, that liar of the first magnitude," was nothing in comparison to me. I must have been twelve years old before my conscience was first awakened up to a sense of the necessity of truth as a principle, as well as its holiness as a virtue. Afterwards, having to set right the minds of others cleared by my own mind on this and some other important points.

I do not think I was naturally obstinate, but remember going without food all day, and being sent hungry and exhausted to bed, because I would not do some trifling thing required of me. I think it was to recite some lines I knew by heart. I was punished as wilfully obstinate: but what no one knew then, and what I know now as the fact, was, that after refusing to do what was required, and bearing anger and threats in consequence, I lost the power to do it. I became stone: the *will* was petrified, and I absolutely *could* not comply. They might have hacked me in pieces before my lips could have unclosed to utterance. The obstinacy was not in the mind, but on the nerves; and I am persuaded that what we call obstinacy in children, and grown-up people, too, is often something of this kind, and that it may be increased by mismanagement, by persistence, or what is called firmness in the controlling power, into disease, or something near to it.

There was in my childish mind another cause of suffering besides those I have mentioned, less acute. but more permanent and always unacknowledged. It was fear

—fear of darkness and supernatural influences. As long as I can remember anything, I remember these horrors of my infancy. How they had been awakened I do not know; they were never revealed. I had heard other children ridiculed for such fears, and held my peace. At first these haunting, thrilling, stifling terrors were vague; afterwards the form varied; but one of the most permanent was the ghost in Hamlet. There was a volume of Shakspeare lying about, in which was an engraving I have not seen since, but it remains distinct in my mind as a picture. On one side stood Hamlet with his hair on end, literally "like quills upon the fretful porcupine," and one hand with all the fingers outspread. On the other strided the ghost, encased in armour with nodding plumes; one finger pointing forwards, and all surrounded with a supernatural light. O, that spectre! for three years it followed me up and down the dark staircase, or stood by my bed: only the blessed light had power to exorcise it. How it was that I knew, while I trembled and quaked, that it was unreal, never cried out, never expostulated, never confessed, I do not know. The figure of Apollyon looming over Christian, which I had found in an old edition of the "Pilgrim's Progress," was also a great torment. But worse, perhaps, were certain phantasms without shape,—things like the vision in Job,—"*A spirit passed before my face; it stood still, but I could not discern the form thereof:*"—and if not intelligible voices, there were strange unaccountable sounds filling the air around with a sort of mysterious life. In daylight I was not only fearless, but audacious, inclined to defy all power and brave all danger,—that is, all danger I could see. I remember volunteering to lead the way through a herd of cattle (among which was a dangerous bull, the terror of the neighbourhood) armed only with a little stick; but first I said the Lord's Prayer fervently. In the ghastly night I never prayed; terror stifled prayer. These visionary sufferings, in some form or other, pursued me till I was nearly twelve years old. If I had not possessed a strong constitution and a strong understanding, which rejected and contemned my own fears, even while they shook me, I had been destroyed. How much weaker children suffer in this way I have since known; and have known how to bring them help and strength, through sympathy and knowledge, the sympathy that soothes and does not encourage—the knowledge that dispels and does not suggest the evil.

People in general, even those who have been much interested in education, are not aware of the sacred duty of *truth*, exact truth in their intercourse with children. Limit what you tell them according to the measure of their faculties; but let what you say be the truth. Accuracy not merely as to fact, but well-considered accuracy in the use of words, is essential with children. I have read some wise book on the treatment of the insane, in which absolute veracity and accuracy in speaking is prescribed as a *curative* principle; and deception for any purpose is deprecated as almost fatal to the health of the patient. Now, it is a good sanitary principle that what is curative is preventive; and that an unhealthy state of mind, leading to madness, may, in some organizations, be induced by that sort of uncertainty and perplexity which grows up where the mind has not been accustomed to truth in its external relations. It is like breathing for a continuance an impure or confined air.

Of the mischief that may be done to a childish mind by a falsehood uttered in thoughtless gayety, I remember an absurd and yet a painful instance. A visitor was turning over for a little girl some prints, one of which represented an Indian widow springing into the fire kindled for the funeral pile of her husband. It was thus explained to the child, who asked innocently whether, if her father died, her mother would be burned? The person to whom the question was addressed, a lively, amiable woman, was probably much amused by the question, and answered giddily, " Oh, of course,—certainly!" and was believed implicitly. But thenceforth, for many weary months, the mind of that child was haunted and tortured by the image of her mother springing into the devouring flames, and consumed by fire, with all the accessories of the picture, particularly the drums beating to drown her cries. In a weaker organization, the results might have been permanent and serious. But to proceed.

These terrors I have described had an existence external to myself: I had no power over them to shape them by my will, and their power over me vanished gradually before a more dangerous infatuation — the propensity to revery. The shaping spirit of imagination began when I was about eight or nine years old to haunt my *inner* life. I can truly say that, from ten years old to fourteen or fifteen, I lived a double existence; one outward, linking me with the external sensible world, the other inward, creating a world to and for itself, conscious to itself only. I carried on for whole years a series of actions, scenes, and adventures; one springing out of another, and coloured and modified by increasing knowledge. This habit grew so upon me, that there were moments—as when I came to some crisis in my imaginary adventures, when I was not more awake to outward things than in sleep—scarcely took cognisance of the beings around me. When punished for idleness by being placed in solitary confinement (the worst of all punishments for children), the intended penance was nothing less than a delight and an emancipation, giving me up to my dreams. I had a very strict and very accomplished governess, one of the cleverest women I have ever met with in my life; but nothing of this was known or even suspected by her, and I exulted in possessing something which her power could not reach. My reveries were my real life: it was an unhealthy state of things.

Those who are engaged in the training of children will perhaps pause here. It may be said, in the first place, How are we to reach those recesses of the inner life which the God who made us keeps from every eye but his own? As when we walk over the field in spring we are aware of a thousand influences and processes at work of which we have no exact knowledge or clear perception, yet must watch and use accordingly; so it is with education. And secondly, it may be asked, if such secret processes be working unconscious mischief, where is the remedy? The remedy is in employment.

Then the mother or the teacher echoes with astonishment, "Employment! the child is employed from morning till night; she is learning a dozen sciences and languages; she has masters and lessons for every hour of every day; with her pencil, her piano, her books, her companions, her birds, her flowers; what can she want more?" An energetic child even at a very early age, and yet further as the physical organization is developed, wants something more and something better; employment which shall bring with it the bond of a higher duty than that which centres in self and self-improvement; employment which shall not merely cultivate the understanding, but strengthen and elevate the conscience; employment for the higher and more generous faculties; employment addressed to the sympathies; employment which has the aim of utility, not pretended, but real, obvious, direct utility. A girl who as a mere child is not always being taught or being amused, whose mind is early restrained by the bond of definite duty, and thrown out of the limit of self, will not in after years be subject to fancies that disturb or to reveries that absorb, and the present and the actual will have that power they ought to have as combined in due degree with desire and anticipation.

DISCRIMINATION WITH RESPECT TO CHILDREN.

From a most excellent volume, entitled "My Mother, or Recollections of Maternal Influence," we take the following plea for little children, and particularly commend it to the attention of mothers.

In the discipline of children, as in all government, it is important to estimate offences according to the degree of their *moral obliquity*. Sins of ignorance, or of inadvertency, of which children commit a great many, are not to be put upon a par with deliberate and downright iniquities—even though the former be more mischievous in their effects (putting *moral* tendencies out of view) than the latter. This is very obvious, but not always acted on. There are parents who will be more disturbed by an accident than by a crime. For instance, they will more severely reprove or punish a child for breaking a looking-glass or a piece of porcelain, than for a falsehood or a quarrel. And what wonder if the child himself learns to estimate his conduct by the same law. An accident alarms him for the consequences, while a moral fault does not distress his conscience. So much *harm* done, so much *guilt;* or rather, so much obnoxiousness to punishment, or blame. An unsuccessful fraud, a lie from which no mischief follows, a fit of anger that injures nobody, is passed over by the parent as though it were venial; and so the child's conscience, as well as his fears, is relieved. Nor is that the worst

His conscience is *mis-instructed*. His moral vision is perverted, and a false standard of accountability and character given him, to take along with him up to manhood, and through life, till the great tribunal of another world sets him right.

You will often see a child attempt to forestall the punishment of an act by offering the parent an equivalent. "How much did the broken thing cost? I will pay you for it out of the money I have got laid up." If the act was one of mere heedlessness, and if such heedlessness was habitual, it might be expedient to take the money, as a means of correcting the heedless habit. The heedlessness of servants is often corrected in this way.

My mother never confounded the venial with the culpable; and I remember instances where, but for such discrimination in her, I might have smarted for doings that only incurred some gentle reproof, as a caution for the future. To give you an example. A cousin having come to see us, my brother and me, one summer day, we amused ourselves a while with observing the bees. The wish arose in our hearts that we had some of their honey. But how to get at it? At length it was suggested that, if a hive were overturned, they would fly away and leave their treasure at our mercy. "Who will upset it, then?" We were all quite young, myself the youngest; and as it generally happens among children that the risks and responsibilities are put upon the youngest, it was proposed to me to perform the feat. I got behind a hive, therefore, and over it went; and you may imagine the music about our ears that ensued thereupon. It was wɔ that flew away, and not the bees. My mother came out, exclaiming at the hazard and the mischief, and, quite contrary to our expectation, said no more about it. Our very ignorance of the risk we ran (for we might have been stung to death) was evidence to her that we had no culpable intentions. She had tho courage to replace the hive, greatly to the contentment of the bees, and had the good fortune to do so without getting stung. Do you know that bees have a special antipathy to some people, and will sting them almost unprovoked, while others can do anything with them with impunity? She was one of their favourites, as they were hers.

I apprehend that we often do injustice to the feelings and behaviour of children by not duly considering that they *are* children. We forget how inexperienced they are, how excitable, how imaginative and impulsive. A friend of ours, in a letter, the other day, described the high excitement of her little daughter, whom she was about to take with her on a visit to some relations. The child ran up stairs and down, flew to the window, as if to anticipate the carriage, and could neither eat nor sleep. "Is it possible," exclaims the mother, "that *I* was ever such an one?" Yes, madam, you were, probably, very much such an one.

Mrs. Howitt, in her "Own Story," tell us that in her childhood she saw on a distant hill-top what seemed to her "an immense elephant, or monstrous beast. I never saw it as anything else," she says. "I was not at all afraid of it, for I saw it every day. Once I said to a visiter, when in a very talkative humour, that a great black elephant always stood opposite to our house. My parents reproved me for saying that which was not true. I stoutly maintained that it was so; my firmness seemed like wilful obstinacy, and I was reproved severely; but I would not withdraw my assertion, and my parents, grieving to see such perversity, thought it much better to let the subject drop. This affair sunk deep in my mind. I saw the elephant every day as plain as could be, but I dared not recur to the subject, because it had given so much displeasure. The fields, however, were bought; and then we went to the very top of them; and as I ascended the hill, my elephant was gone, there was nothing at all but two dark Scotch firs, and a slender ash-tree growing beside them. [The trunks and tops of the firs forming the legs and body of the creature, and the ash tree head and proboscis, aided by the obscurity of the English atmosphere, which is much less clear than ours.] The whole thing was disenchanted; and when I returned home, though I still, by a stretch of the imagination, could see the elephant, it gradually became three distinct trees. I never, as I remember, mentioned it to any one, not even to Anna, but it made a deep impression on my mind, and has given me great charity with the exaggerations and even the apparent falsehoods of children."

Truth, strict truth, is certainly to be inculcated. The slightest deviations from it should alarm us, and put us upon correcting so pernicious a habit. There can be no true excellence of character—there is no foundation for it, without integrity. Behold an Israelite indeed, in whom is *no guile.* Even the honest exaggerations of a lively imagination ought to be checked, lest they lead to something worse. Yet, mere misapprehensions, elephants made out of trees, are not to be treated as wilful whole-cloth falsehoods.

When I see how very strict and strait-laced some people are with children, I feel disposed to put in a plea or two in their behalf. Pray be a little tolerant of our mirth and noise, because of the excess of our animal spirits; which we can no more repress wholly than you can stop the gushing fountains and flowing brooks of spring. How delightful to all young creatures is freedom! Pray suffer us to breathe a little of that wholesome luxury. Why should we be made to envy the lambs that frolic in the pastures? What! is our home a monastery, and are we monks and nuns, that *nowhere* and *never* can we for a moment seem to ourselves exempt from irksome supervision—never feel ourselves at large a little, to run about as our eager senses and our sportive spirits prompt us? How absurd to say to us, as you often do in look and in effect, if not in just those words, "Don't be so childish!" What are we else but children, and what else is to be expected but that we should think as children, speak as children, and understand and act as children? When we become men and women we shall behave as such. You wonder at our emotions and behaviour; you see nothing to justify it. We are always looking, hearkening, shouting, leaping, wishing, fearing, hoping, in the midst of the most ordinary objects. Well, we have to say to you that the most ordinary things are new and strange to us, and therefore exciting. Do but consider that that mountain there—hill or hillock only, as it may seem to you—over which the blue sky sleeps, or the fleecy clouds sail, is the first, perhaps the only like elevation we ever saw, and saw that so recently that it does not yet cease to affect us with a feeling of the sublime. To you it is a fixed and motionless object; but to us its top nods and swims, as if it were going to topple down, or sail away. High trees, tall steeples, great rocks, deep pits and gullies, dark fathomless wells, frightful precipices, awful solitudes, great storms and floods, roaring winds and cataracts, loud thunder, lightnings that can be felt upon the hands and face, unutterable splendours in the rainbow—these and such like things, how few of them you seem to perceive at your time of life; but we, all sensitive, and wakeful, and inexperienced as we are, are meeting with them continually. We see a thousand sights you do not see, and hear a thousand sounds you do not hear. How alive to us the air is with birds! how social the woods with winged creatures, quadrupeds, and creeping things! A squirrel arrests and amuses us as a mastodon would hardly arrest you. What an incident to us is the passage of the wild geese screaming along their airy way mid-heaven! Do you see how vexed the sunbeams are with insects? You heed them not; you even brush them from your eyes and breathe with scarce a consciousness of their presence. What a saucy rogue is echo! How startling is the sudden singing of the locust; and what a din the beetle makes upon the wing! What mysterious things the fire-flies are, twinkling in the dark: and how wakeful does the distant baying of the mastiff keep us, when we have gone to bed! A love of the marvellous we confess. It is natural alike to us and you, with this difference, that with you experience has done away with the objects that used to excite it.

Some such plea as this I incline to make in behalf of such little people as are subjected to uncharitable judgment, or over-strict restraint. A still child is either unwell or unnatural; and a child that sees things with the senses of an adult is either a prodigy or a dolt. The eyes of children are magnifying lenses, and their ears acoustic tubes. They see things large and wonderful, and see them manifold and multiform—a hundred cats where there are but two or three. Hence the cumulative style of their descriptions—"great, big, large"—with all the other intensive words and synonyms they are able to command; and hence we often charge them, and sometimes cruelly, perhaps, with culpable exaggerations, if not with downright falsehoods, when they do but report things as they apprehend them. Hyperbole with them is not hyperbole, in all cases. Do we not all naturally use such language as our senses and emotions dictate? And who shall acquit us grown people of expressing more, or expressing less, than the truth, if other people's senses and experience are to be the standard?

An intelligent gentleman, who had been absent above fifty years from his and our native place, requested my brother to conduct him to the "Beggar-land." This was a little common, a rood or more of green-sward, elliptical in form, with a bank round its sides. It had been a favourite play-ground of several generations On coming to the spot, "*That* the Beggar-land!" he exclaimed. "But how extravagant were my impressions of it! carried away with me in my childhood. I imagined those banks to be at least seventy feet high, and would almost have taken my oath of it; whereas they are not above a dozen feet. And they cannot but be as high now as they ever were, indeed they must be higher; for the level turf is as it was, while the road on one side and the little water-course on the other would naturally be wearing deeper, and thus increase the elevation between."

Thus we see things in our childhood; and due allowance should be made for it, in justice and in charity. However, these remarks must not be pushed too far. While we teach the heart to *mean* truth, we should also discipline the senses to *perceive* the truth; that so the heart, the senses, and the tongue, may all be truthful. How amiable is truthfulness, how beautiful is truth!

HOME ECONOMY.

Mrs. Sigourney, in her admirable series of letters to mothers, offers, on this subject, some truthful observations. She says:—

I have a few words to say to mothers on a point of domestic economy. In a country like ours, where there are few large estates, and where almost every father of a family is subjected to some kind of labour, either for the maintenance of those who are dear, or the preservation of possessions on which they are to depend when he shall be taken from them, the duty of the "helpmeet," to lighten as far as possible these burdens, by a consistent economy, is too obvious to need illustration. To adapt whatever may be intrusted to her care, to the best ends, and to make it subservient to the greatest amount of good, should be her daily study. There is, perhaps, no community of women, who more faithfully, or dexterously, than the wives and mothers of New England, carry this wisdom and forethought into all the details of that science by which the table is spread, and the apparel adapted, to the ever-changing seasons. The same judgment which so admirably regulates food and clothing, it would be desirable to apply to another and a higher department. It is to mothers, with the care of young children, that these remarks on economy are peculiarly addressed. They have the charge of immortal beings, whose physical, mental, and moral temperament are, for a long period, exclusively in their hands. Nothing save the finger of God has written on the tablet, when it is committed to them. It is important that they secure *time* to form deep and lasting impressions.

Let them, therefore, devote their first strength, and their utmost effort, to the highest duties. The heart soon develops itself, and asks culture. Through the feelings and affections it bursts forth, even while the infant is considered not to have advanced beyond animal nature. The preferences, the passions, reveal themselves, like the young tendrils of the vine, reaching out feebly and blindly. The mother must be assiduous, in teaching them where to twine. While the character of the babe is forming, let every action and indication of motive be a subject of observation. But how can she be adequate to this, if the whole attention to the personal comfort of several young children devolves upon herself? If she is to make and mend their articles of dress, bear them in her arms during their period of helplessness, and exhaust herself by toils throughout the day, and watchings by night, how can she have leisure to study their varying shades of disposition, and adapt to each the fitting mode of discipline, as the skilful gardener suits the plant to the soil? Will she not be sometimes moved to apostrophize them, like the leader of the wandering, repining Israelites, "how can I *alone* bear your cumbrance, and your burden, and your strife?"

The remedy is, for the mother to provide herself with competent assistance, in the sphere of manual labour, that she may be enabled to become the constant directress of her children, and have leisure to be happy in their companionship. This would seem to be a rational economy. The thrifty village-matron, when she returns from church, takes off her Sunday dress, and deposits it in its accustomed place, substituting one better fitted to her household duties. She is not blamed for preserving her most valuable garment for its appropriate uses. Let every mother pay herself the same respect, which the good farmer's lady pays her "bettermost gown" not the homage of a miserly parsimony, but a just protection in freshness and order, for fitting and dignified offices.

"My husband cannot afford to hire a nurse for the little ones," said a young friend. "We have so many, that we must economize."

Her mother suggested that the expenditure should be saved in some other department of housekeeping, in the toilette, or in luxurious entertainment. But the counsel was not accepted by the daughter, who, in her zeal for economy, failed to comprehend its elementary principles.

She commenced her task with vigour, and confidence in the correctness of her own decision. Sickness in the various forms that mark the progress of dentition, and neglect of slight diseases in their first symptoms, came upon her young family. Uninstructed by experience, she gave powerful medicines for trifling maladies, or summoned and teased physicians, when Nature was simply perfecting her own operations. The children who had emerged from infancy, were indulging bad dispositions, and acquiring improper habits. She knew it. But what could she do? She was depressed by fatigue. The wardrobe of her numerous little ones continually required her attention. It would not do for them to be unfashionably clad, or appear worse than their neighbours. So, the soul being most out of sight, must suffer most. Blindness to evil, or hasty punishment, rendering it still more inveterate, were the only resources of her hurried and hurrying mode of existence. For her, there seemed no rest. If health returned to her young family, mental diseases were disclosed. She became spiritless, nervous, and discouraged. She was harassed by the application of force among the inferior machinery. When it was necessary that power should be brought to bear upon the *minds* committed to her care, she was painfully conscious that her energies had spent themselves in other channels. Running up the shrouds like a ship-boy, the helm, where she should stand, was left unguided. The pilot, steering among rocks, does not weary himself with the ropes and rigging, which a common sailor as well manages, and better understands.

The temper and constitution of the young mother became equally impaired. Her husband complained of the bad conduct and rude manners of the children. 'What could she do? She was sure there was nothing but toil and trouble, by night and by day." This was true. There was an error in economy. The means were not adapted to their highest ends. She was an educated woman, and a Christian. Her children should have reaped the advantage of her internal wealth, as soon as their unfolding minds cast forth the first beam of intelligence. But she led. the life of a galley-slave, and their heritage was in proportion.

Is this an uncommon example? Have we not often witnessed it? Have we not ourselves exhibited some of its lineaments?

The proposed remedy, is to employ an efficient person in the nurse's department. I say *efficient*, for the young girls, to whom this responsibility is sometimes intrusted, are themselves an additional care. "I am not willing," said a judicious father, " to place my infant in the arms of one, with whom I would not trust an expensive glass dish." Half-grown girls are not the proper assistants to a young mother. They themselves need her superintendence, and create new demands on time already too much absorbed.

"I know she is small," says the mistaken parent, "but she will do to *hold a baby.*"

Holding a baby, is not so slight a vocation as many suppose. Physicians assert that deformity is often produced, by keeping an infant in those uneasy positions to which a feeble arm resorts; and health and life have been sacrificed to accidents and falls, through the carelessness, or impatience, of an over-wearied girl. The argument for the substitution of an immature nurse, drawn from the circumstance of the saving of expense, is doubtless futile; for the apparel and means of education, which a conscientious person feels bound to provide for a young girl, will equal the wages of a woman. In many departments of domestic labour, the help of minors is both pleasant and profitable; and the lady who brings them up properly, confers a benefit on the community, and may secure to herself lasting gratitude and attachment.

But the physical welfare of infancy is of such immense importance, that it seems desirable that those whom the mother associates with herself in this department, should have attained full strength, both of mind and body. Moral integrity, patient and kind dispositions, industrious habits, and religious principles, are essential to the faithful discharge of these deputed duties, and to render that influence safe, which they will necessarily acquire over the little being whose comfort they promote. Such qualities are deserving of respect, in whatever station they may be found; and I would suggest, both as a point of policy and justice, the attaching higher consideration to the office of a nurse, when her character comprises them. If the nurture of an immortal being for immortality is an honourable work, and if its earliest impressions are allowed to be most indelible, those who minister to its humblest wants, partake in some measure of its elevated destiny; as the porters and Levites derived dignity from the temple-service, though they might not wear the Urim and Thummim of the High-Priest, or direct the solemn sacrifices, when the flame of Heaven descended upon the altar.

To the inquiry, why this kind of assistance is more needed by the mother in our own days, than by her of the "olden time," by whom the care of children, the operations of the needle, the mysteries of culinary science, and all the complicated duties of housekeeping, were simultaneously performed, without failure or chasm, the natural reply is, that the structure of society is different, and from an educated parent the modern system of division of labour asks new and extended effort. She requires aid, not that she may indulge in indolence, but that she may devote the instruments intrusted to her to their legitimate uses. There is, perhaps, no sphere of action, where indolence is both so fatal and so sinful, as in that of a mother of young children. She is a sentinel who should never sleep at her post. She cannot be long relieved without hazard, or exchanged without loss. She should therefore be careful of her strength, her health, and her life, *for her children's sake*. If she employ a subaltern, it is that she may give herself more exclusively to their highest and best interests.

Let her be persuaded, whatever may be the demands upon her time, or their advantages for gaining knowledge from other sources, *to spend systematically a portion of time in their daily instruction.* Let her also be with them, when they retire at night, to review the day's little gatherings and doings, and to point the tender spirit to the Giver of all its gifts. Let the period devoted to them, be as far as possible uninterrupted by the presence of others, and chosen, in the morning, before care has seized the teacher's mind, or temptation sadden the beloved pupil. Let the time be spent in reading some book adapted to their comprehension, which conveys useful knowledge or moral and religious instruction, questioning them respecting its contents, and adding such illustrations, as the subject, or their peculiar state of intellect and feeling, may render appropriate; having it always understood, that at night, some recapitulation will be expected of the lessons of the day.

The mother who regularly does this, will find herself in the practice of a true and palpable economy. She will be induced to furnish herself with new knowledge, and to simplify it, for those whom she seeks to train up for the kingdom of heaven. She will not strive to combine fashionable amusement, or dissipation of thought, with her solemn and delightful obligations. She will labour as "ever in her Great Task-Master's Eye," to do for the minds and souls of her children, that which none can perform as well as herself, which, if she neglects, may not be done at all, and which, if left undone, will be a loss, for which Eternity must pay.

YOUNG MOTHER.

Young mother, what do you hold in your arms? A machine of exquisite symmetry; the blue veins revealing the mysterious life-tide through an almost transparent surface; the waking thought speaking through the sparkling eye, or dissolving there in tears; such a form as the art of man has never equalled; and such a union of matter with mind, as his highest reason fails to comprehend. You embrace a being, whose developments may yet astonish you; who may perhaps sway the destiny of others; whose gatherings of knowledge you can neither foresee nor limit; and whose chequered lot of sorrow or of joy. are known only to the Omnipotence which fashioned him. Still, if this were all, the office of a mother would lose its crowning dignity. But to be the guide of a spirit which can never die, to make the first indelible impressions on what may be a companion of seraphs, and live with an unbounded capacity for bliss or woe, when these poor skies under which it was born, shall have vanished like a vision, this is the fearful honour which God hath intrusted to the "weaker vessel," and which would make us tremble amid our happiness, if we took not refuge in Him.

I have seen a young and beautiful mother, herself like a brilliant and graceful flower. Nothing could divide her from her infant. It was to her as a twin-soul. She had loved society, for there she had been as an idol. But what was the fleeting delight of adulation, to the deep love that took possession of her whole being! She had loved her father's house. There, she was ever like a song-bird, the first to welcome the day, and the last to bless it. Now, she wreathed the same blossoms of the heart around another home, and lulled her little nursling with the same inborn melodies.

It was sick. She hung over it. She watched it. She comforted it. She sat whole nights with it in her arms. It was to her like the beloved of the King of Israel, "feeding among the lilies." Under the pressure of this care, there was in her eye a deep and holy beauty, which never gleamed there, when she was radiant in the dance, or in the halls of fashion the cynosure. She had been taught to love God, and his worship, from her youth up; but when health again glowed in the face of her babe, there came from her lip such a prayer of flowing praise, as it had never before breathed.

And when in her beautiful infant there were the first developments of character, and of those preferences and aversions which leave room to doubt whether they are from simplicity or perverseness, and whether they should be repressed or pitied, and how the harp might be so tuned as not to injure its tender and intricate harmony, there burst from her soul a supplication more earnest, more self-abandoning, more prevailing, than she had ever before poured into the ear of the majesty of Heaven.

So the feeble hand of the babe that she nourished, led her through more profound depths of humility, to higher aspirations of faith. And I felt that the affection, to whose hallowed influence she had so yielded, was guiding her to a higher seat among the "just made perfect."

HOW TO MAKE BOYS LOVE HOME.

"I WISH those boys loved to stay at home in the evening," said a mother in my hearing, last night; and the sigh and look of distress which accompanied her words, told plainly that her heart was deeply pained by their oft-repeated absence, and she watched their retreating footsteps with a troubled countenance, and knew not what might be the company they sought, nor what evil influence might be thrown around them.

They were industrious boys of sixteen and eighteen, just beginning to fancy they were too large and too old to be longer subject to parental authority. They were not vicious or idle, but worked with a willing hand through the day, doing the work of men; but when evening came, they sought pleasure abroad, unmindful of a father's advice, or a mother's entreaty. I glanced around their home, a comfortable, farmer-like dwelling, where all the wants of the physical nature were well supplied, but, as is too often the case, the food for the mind was less abundant. A few school books, which the boys had never learned to love, a Bible, and a hymn book, constituted the family library; and I was not surprised that they should leave the circle at home, and seek the cheerful throng that were lounging in the store, or join in the vulgar mirth and profane jests that went round the boisterous group.

"You are seeing your happiest days with your boy,"

said the mother to me, as my baby clung to my arm with the sweet confidence of infancy; "you know *where he is*, and have no anxiety for him now; but when he is older, he will be beyond your influence, and go you know not where."

I thought of the old proverb, "Train up a child in the way he should go, and when he is old he will not depart from it;" and I shook my head doubtingly, and said nothing. But I asked myself, is it really true, as I have often heard it remarked, that parents enjoy more pleasure in the society of their children in infancy, than in youth and maturity? If so, surely there is a reason, and that reason too often the result of parental mistakes in the early discipline of their children. We watch with delight the first dawning of intellect, await with impatience the first indistinct effort to talk, and are pleased with their infantile prattle, and it seems strange that the pleasures of social intercourse should diminish with their growing intelligence.

But we cannot expect children to be like ourselves, steady, old, and care-worn. Fun and frolic are essential to their happiness, and it is no injury to any one to join heartily in these sports. If we enter into their sports in childhood, and take the lead of their pleasures in youth, we shall keep our own hearts young and joyous, make home the centre of attractions, and while doing much to educate their mental faculties, we shall find a far greater satisfaction in their society, than we can possibly find in the artless trust of infancy.

A few dollars judiciously expended in books and engravings suitable for young children, will do much to awaken a love of home; and I venture to assert, there is nothing which will have a stronger influence in keeping "those boys" quietly at home, than to cultivate a *taste for reading.* Begin early. Read to them before they can read for themselves; explain what you read, and encourage them to converse with you about it. Teach them to observe the common phenomena of nature, and to study into the causes which produce the effects they see. A mother may do this herself without being a philosopher. She may awaken their curiosity upon the various objects around them, and direct them where this curiosity may be gratified, place within their reach useful and instructive books, and show by example as well as by precept that she appreciates them, and the pleasures of home will be purer and sweeter to every member of the family, and the children will seldom have occasion to seek evening amusement away from the charmed circle of home. It has been truthfully said, "a good book is the best of company;" and the earlier we introduce our children into the society of *good books*, the greater will be the benefit derived from them, and the stronger will be their attachment to the social circle around the evening fire, and there will be less danger of their seeking diversion in the society of the idle and vicious. But if we neglect to make home happy, and to furnish entertainment for the intellect, be assured that the restless desire of the human mind for "some new thing," will frequently attract "those boys," and girls too, away from home in search of amusement.

HAPPY AT HOME.

Let the gay and the idle go forth where they will,
In search of soft Pleasure, that syren of ill;
Let them seek her in Fashion's illumined saloon,
Where Melody mocks at the heart out of tune;
Where the laugh gushes light from the lips of the maiden
While her spirit, perchance, is with sorrow o'erladen;
And where, 'mid the garlands Joy only should braid,
Is Slander, the snake, by its rattle betrayed.
Ah, no! let the idle for happiness roam,
For me—I but ask to be "happy at home!"

At home! oh how thrillingly sweet is that word,
And by it what visions of beauty are stirred!
I ask not that Luxury curtain my room
With damask from India's exquisite loom;
The sunlight of heaven is precious to me,
And muslin will veil it if blazing too free;
The elegant trifles of Fashion and Wealth
I need not—I ask but for comfort and health!
With these and my dear ones I care not to roam,
For, oh! I am happy, most "happy at home!"

One bright little room where the children may play,
Unfearful of spoiling the costly array;
Where he, too—our dearest of all on the earth,
May find the sweet welcome he loves at his hearth;
The fire blazing warmly—the sofa drawn nigh,
And the star lamp alight on the table close by;
A few sunny pictures in simple frames shrined,
A few precious volumes—the wealth of the mind;
And here and there treasured some rare gem of art,
To kindle the fancy or soften the heart;
Thus richly surrounded, why, why should I roam?
Oh! am I not happy—most "happy at home?"

The little ones, weary of books and of play,
Nestle down on our bosoms—our Ellen and May!
And softly the simple, affectionate prayer,
Ascends in the gladness of innocence there;
And now, ere they leave us, sweet kisses and light
They lavish, repeating their merry "good-night!"
While I with my needle, my book, or my pen,
Or in converse with Him, am contented again,
And cry—"Can I ever be tempted to roam,
While blessings like these make me happy at home?"

OUR OLD GRANDMOTHER.

Blessed be the children who have an old-fashioned grandmother! As they hope for length of days let them love and honour her, for we can tell them they will never find another.

The dear, old-fashioned grandmother, whose thread of love, spun "by hand" on life's little wheel, was longer and stronger than they make it now, was wound about and about the children she saw playing in the children's arms, in a true love knot that nothing but the shears of Atropos could sever; for do we not recognise the lambs sometimes, when summer days are over, and autumn winds are blowing, as they come bleating from the yellow fields, by the crimson thread we wound about their necks in April or May, and so undo the gate and let the wanderers in?

There is a large old kitchen somewhere in the past, and an old-fashioned fire-place therein, with its smooth old jambs of stone; smooth with many knives that had been sharpened there; smooth with many little fingers that have clung there. There are andirons, too, the old andirons, with rings in the top, wherein many temples of flames have been builded, with spires and turrets of crimson. There is a broad worn hearth; broad enough for three generations to cluster on; worn by feet that have been torn and bleeding by the way, or been made "beautiful," and walked upon floors of tessellated gold. There are tongs in the corner wherewith we grasped a coal, and "blowing for a little life," lighted our first candle; there is a shovel, wherewith were drawn forth the glowing embers in which we saw our first fancies and dreamed our first dreams; the shovel with which we stirred the sleepy logs till the sparks rushed up the chimney, as if a forge were in blast below, and wished we had so many lambs, or so many marbles, or so many somethings that we coveted; and so it was we wished our first wishes.

There is a chair—a low, rush-bottom chair; there is a little wheel in the corner, a big wheel in the garret, a loom in the chamber. There are chests full of linen and yarn, and quilts of rare pattern, and "samplers" in frames.

And everywhere and always the dear old wrinkled face of her whose firm, elastic step mocks the feeble saunter of her children's children—the old-fashioned grandmother of twenty years ago. She, the very Providence of the old homestead; she, who loved us all, and said she wished there were more of us to love, and took all the school in the Hollow for grandchildren beside. A great expansive heart was hers, beneath that woollen gown, or that more stately bombazine, or that sole heirloom of silken texture.

We can see her to-day, those mild blue eyes, with more of beauty in them than Time could touch or Death do more than hide—those eyes that held both smiles and tears within the faintest call of every one of us, and soft reproof, that seemed not passion but regret. A white tress has escaped from beneath her snowy cap; she has just restored a wandering lamb to its mother; she lengthened the tether of a vine that was straying over a window, as she came in, and plucked a four-leaved clover for Ellen. She sits down by the little wheel—a tress is running through her fingers from the distaff's dishevelled head, when a small voice cries "Grandma," from the old red cradle, and "Grandma!" Tommy shouts from the top of the stairs. Gently she lets go the thread, for her patience is almost as beautiful as her charity, and she touches the little red bark a moment till the young voyager is in a dream again, and then directs Tommy's unavailing attempts to harness the cat. The tick of the clock runs faint and low, and she opens the mysterious door and proceeds to wind it up. We are all on tiptoe, and we beg in a breath to be lifted up and look in for the hundredth time upon the tin cases of the weights, and the poor lonely pendulum, which goes to and fro by its little dim window, and never comes out in the world; and our petitions are all granted, and we are lifted up, and we all touch with a finger the wonderful weights, and the music of the little wheel is resumed.

Was Mary to be married, or Jane to be wrapped in a

shroud? So meekly did she fold the white hands of the one upon her still bosom, that there seemed to be a prayer in them there; and so sweetly did she wreath the white rose in the hair of the other, that one would not have wondered had more roses budded for company.

How she stood between us and apprehended harm; how the rudest of us softened beneath the gentle pressure of her faded and tremulous hand! From her capacious pocket that hand was ever withdrawn closed, only to be opened in our own with the nuts she had gathered, the cherries she had plucked, the little egg she had found, the "turn-over" she had baked, the trinket she had purchased for us as the product of her spinning, the blessing she had stored for us—the offspring of her heart.

What treasures of story fell from those old lips! of good fairies and evil; of the old times when she was a girl; and we wondered if ever—but then she couldn't be handsomer or dearer, but that she ever was "little." And then, when we begged her to sing, "Sing us one of the good old songs you used to sing to mother, grandma."

"Children, I can't sing," she always said; and mother used to lay her knitting softly down, and the kitten stopped playing with the yarn upon the floor, and the clock ticked lower in the corner, and the fire died down to a glow like an old heart that is neither chilled nor dead, and grandmother sang. To be sure it wouldn't do for the parlour and the concert-room now-a-days; but then it was the old kitchen, and the old-fashioned grandmother, and the old ballad, in the dear old times, and we can hardly see to write for the memory of them, though it is hand's breadth to the sunset.

Well, she sang. Her voice was feeble and wavering, like a fountain just ready to fall, but then how sweet-toned it was; and it became deeper and stronger, but it couldn't grow sweeter. What "joy of grief" it was to sit there around the fire, all of us except Jane; that clasped a prayer to her bosom, and her we thought we saw when the hall door was opened a moment by the wind; but then we were not afraid, for wasn't it her old smile she wore?—to sit there around the fire and weep over the woes of the "Babes in the Woods," who lay down side by side in the great solemn shadows; and how strangely glad we felt when the robin red-breast covered them with leaves, and last of all when the angels took them out of the night into day-everlasting.

We may think what we will of it now, but the song and the story heard around the kitchen fire have coloured the thoughts and lives of the most of us; have given us the germs of whatever poetry blesses our hearts; whatever of memory blooms in our yesterdays. Attribute whatever we may to the school and the schoolmaster, the rays which make that little day we call life radiate from the God-swept circle of the hearth-stone.

Then she sings an old lullaby she sang to mother— *her* mother sang to her; but she does not sing it through, and falters ere 'tis done. She rests her head upon her hands, and it is silent in the old kitchen. Something glitters down between her fingers in the fire-light, and it looks like rain in the soft sunshine. The old grandmother is thinking when she first heard the song, and of the voice that sang it; when, a light-haired and light-hearted girl, she hung around that mother's chair, nor saw the shadows of the years to come. Oh! the days that are no more! What spell can we weave to bring them back again? What words unsay, what deeds undo, to set back, just this once, the ancient clock of time?

So all our little hands were for ever clinging to her garments and staying her, as if from dying, for long ago she had done living for herself, and lived alone in us. But the old kitchen wants a presence to-day, and the rush-bottomed chair is tenantless.

How she used to welcome us when we were grown, and came back once more to the homestead.

We *thought* we were men and women, but we were children there. The old-fashioned grandmother was blind in the eyes, but she saw with her heart, as she always did. We threw our long shadows through the door, and she felt them as they fell over her form, and she looked dimly up and saw tall shapes in the doorway, and she says, "Edward I know, and Lucy's voice I can hear, but who is the other? It must be Jane's;" for she had almost forgotten the folded hands. "Oh, no! not Jane; for she—let me see—she is waiting for me, isn't she?" and the old grandmother wandered and wept.

"It is another daughter, grandmother, that Edward has brought," says some one, "for your blessing."

"Has she blue eyes, my son? Put her hand in mine, for she is my latest born, the child of my old age. Shall I sing you a song, children?" Her hand is in her pocket as of old; she is idly fumbling for a toy, a welcome gift for the children that have come again.

One of us, men as we thought we were, is weeping; she hears the half-suppressed sob; she says,

"Here, my poor child, rest upon your grandmother's shoulder; she will protect you from all harm. Come, children, sit round the fire again. Shall I sing you a song or tell you a story? Stir the fire, for it is cold; the nights are growing colder!"

The clock in the corner struck nine, the bedtime of those old days. The song of life was indeed sung, the story told; it was bedtime at last. Good night to thee, grandmother! The old-fashioned grandmother was no more, and we miss her for ever. But we will set up a tablet in the midst of the memory, in the midst of the heart, and write on it only this: "Sacred to the Memory of the old-fashioned Grandmother. God bless her for ever!"

GOVERNMENT OF CHILDREN.

ANTICIPATE and prevent fretfulness and ill-temper by keeping the child in good health, ease, and comfort. Never quiet with giving to eat, or by bribing in any way, still less by opiates.

For the first few months avoid loud and harsh sounds in the hearing of children, or violent lights in their sight; address them in soft tones; do nothing to frighten them; and never jerk or roughly handle them.

Avoid angry words and violence both to a child and in its presence: by which means a naturally violent child may be trained to gentleness.

Moderate any propensity of a child, such as anger, violence, greediness for food, cunning, &c., which appears too active. Show him no example of these.

Let the mother be, and let her select servants such as she wishes the child to be. The youngest child is affected by the conduct of those in whose arms he lives.

Let a mother *feel as she ought*, and she will *look as she feels*. Much of a child's earliest moral training is by looks and gestures.

When necessary, exhibit firmness and authority, always with perfect temper, composure, and self-possession.

Never give a child that which it cries for; and avoid being too ready in answering children's demands, else they become impatient of refusal, and selfish.

When the child is most violent, the mother should be most calm and silent. Out-screaming a screaming child is as useless as it is mischievous. Steady denial of the object screamed for, is the best cure for screaming.

In such contests, witnesses should withdraw, and leave mother and child alone. A child is very ready to look round and attract the aid of *foreign* sympathy in its little rebellions.

Never promise to give when the child leaves off crying. Let the crying be the reason for *not* giving.

SPECIAL EDUCATION.

True education in its highest sense is, as we have again and again remarked, the thorough and happy development of the whole nature. It is not the mere acquisition of knowledge, of accomplishments, of manners—it is not the cultivation of the intellect or of the heart, but it is the blending of all these means for the attainment of one grand end—an end to be arrived at by silent and almost imperceptible degrees.

To suppose that education can be completed within a given number of years and lessons, to imagine that by the aid of masters on the one side, and a certain amount of daily application on the other, a man or woman will become as finished as a Dutch painting, or the miniatures of Sacci, is a popular fallacy, which must be exploded before long.

Knowledge and wisdom are often confounded in conversation and in books, so, too, are instruction and education; but a little thought—a very little will serve to expose the delusion. In advocating a large and liberal system of education, we are not, by any means, disposed to overlook the specialities of instruction. For many peculiar spheres, peculiar knowledge is required. A comprehensive view of things, and the power of extracting great principles from a number of small details, betoken a well-cultivated mind; but it will be manifestly defective if from this mental height it cannot descend to the daily duties and solicitudes, the necessary acts and acquisitions, of every-day existence.

Cloud-land, however gorgeous, is not the home for frail, helpless human souls; the sphere of noble and invigorating thought, the fairy land of poetry, the seductive regions of romance, the peaceful haunts cf contemplation, must only be resorted to, in order that from them we may gain fresh vigour for life's common cares. It is not difficult to draw a picture of the accomplished young lady, who is admirably fitted for shining in society, and perfectly unadapted for the trials and emergencies of domestic life.

But it is possible—and to this point we wish to draw special attention—that the highly accomplished, but ill-educated woman may be merely on a level with one of great intellectual endowments and culture in the fulfilment of her domestic duties. Both may be equally ignorant, equally without training, and equally incompetent to manage a household, to direct servants, to attend either to the physical or moral education of their children. The one has spent her maiden-life in those pursuits which prove attractive in society, the other has passed hers, perhaps, in acquiring information, in developing her mental powers, in earnest thought on great and earnest subjects—both, from very different causes, are alike deficient in that special knowledge which every woman should acquire.

It is scarcely necessary to point out in what this knowledge consists. A few suggestive hints and instances will, however, not be out of place.

There are few women who do not learn how to train

and treat their servants, by means of a good deal of awkward and unpleasant experience. There are some who betray their incapacity, and testify to their annoyance in consequence through the whole of their housekeeping existence. Every fault is laid upon the domestics; it never occurs to them that their own conduct is defective, that they expect more than can be reasonably hoped for, or by their uncertain and fitful caprices forfeit the respect and irritate the temper of their servants.

To exercise authority without abusing it, to hold the reins with a firm and yet a gentle hand, and to win the affections of her servants without encouraging familiarity, is an art which all ladies should learn, not only for the sake of their own comfort, but out of consideration to those who serve under them.

How to nurse sick children is another problem which the most loving and feminine intuition will not solve. It needs special knowledge, which must first of all be gained from books and then from careful practice.

The knowledge of the laws of health, of the means by which the physical powers are developed, and of everything that is detrimental to the frame, however sanctioned by fashion or custom, should be especially urged upon the attention of women. Where health is concerned, women are frequently more inconsiderate and careless than men. They fancy they may commit almost any act of folly, and yet escape with impunity. Often a life-long illness is the penalty they have to pay for this wilful ignorance.

Then, again, women should have a general acquaintance with the different articles of food, and with their different prices; they should know where to buy with advantage; and the science of economy is one in which, without any hints from their husbands, they should be perfectly at home. It would be easy to add a whole string of requisitions which we are inclined to demand from well-educated women. But we have only space to repeat our assertion that, combined with that general education which is to be primarily sought after, special knowledge must be added if, as wife or mother, a woman would fill the post assigned her with dignity and success.

FAULT-FINDING.

Mr. Abbott, in his "Mother at Home," makes these judicious remarks on fault-finding. They are commended to the consideration of all who have the government of children:—

Do not be continually finding fault with your children. It is at times necessary to censure and to punish. But very much more may be done by encouraging children when they do well. Be therefore more careful to express your approbation of good conduct, than your disapprobation of bad. Nothing can more discourage a child than a spirit of incessant fault-finding, on the part of its parent. And hardly anything can exert a more injurious influence upon the disposition both of the parent and the child. There are two great motives influencing human actions, hope and fear. Both of these are at times necessary. But who would not prefer to have her child influenced to good conduct by the desire of pleasing, rather than by the fear of offending? If a mother never expresses her gratification when her children do well, and is always censuring them when she sees anything amiss, they are discouraged and unhappy. They feel that it is useless to try to please. Their dispositions become hardened and soured by this ceaseless fretting; and at last, finding that, whether they do well or ill, they are equally found fault with, they relinquish all efforts to please, and become heedless of reproaches.

But let a mother approve of her child's conduct whenever she can. Let her show that his good behaviour makes her sincerely happy. Let her reward him for his efforts to please, by smiles and affection. In this way she will cherish in her child's heart some of the noblest and most desirable feelings of our nature. She will cultivate in him an amiable disposition and a cheerful spirit. Your child has been, during the day, very pleasant and obedient. Just before putting him to sleep for the night, you take his hand and say, " My son, you have been a very good boy to-day. It makes me very happy to see you so kind and obedient. God loves children who are dutiful to their parents, and he promises to make them happy." This approbation from his mother is, to him, a great reward. And when, with a more than ordinarily affectionate tone, you say, " Good night, my dear son," he leaves the room with his little heart full of feeling. And when he closes his eyes for sleep, he is happy, and resolves that he will always try to do his duty.

Basil Hall thus describes the effects produced on board ship, by the different modes of government adopted by different commanders.

"Whenever one of these commanding officers," speaking of a fault-finding captain, "came on board the ship, after an absence of a day or two, and likewise when he made his periodical round of the decks after breakfast, his constant habit was to cast his eye about him, in order to discover what was wrong; to detect the smallest thing that was out of its place; in a word, to find as many grounds for censure as possible. This constituted, in his opinion, the best preventive to neglect, on the part of those under his command; and he acted in this trusty way on principle. The attention of the other officer, on the contrary, appeared to be directed chiefly to those points which he could approve of. For instance, he would stop as he went along, from time to time, and say to the first lieutenant, 'Now, these ropes are very nicely arranged; this mode of stowing the men's bags and mess kids is just as I wish to see it;' while the officer first described would not only pass by these well-arranged things, which had cost hours of labour to put in order, quite unnoticed, but would not be easy till his eye had caught hold of some casual omission which afforded an opening for disapprobation.

"One of these captains would remark to the first lieutenant, as he walked along, 'How white and clean you have got the decks to-day! I think you must have been at them all the morning, to have got them into such order.' The other, in similar circumstances, but eager to find fault, would say, even if the decks were as white and clean as drifted snow, 'I wish you would teach these sweepers to clear away that bundle of shakings!' pointing to a bit of rope yarn not half an inch long, left under the truck of a gun. It seemed, in short, as if nothing was more vexatious to one of these officers, than to discover things so correct as to afford him no good opportunity for finding fault; while, to the other, the necessity of censuring really appeared a punishment to himself.

"Under the one, accordingly, we all worked with cheerfulness, from a conviction that nothing we did in a proper way would miss approbation.

"But our duty under the other, being performed in fear, seldom went on with much spirit. We had no personal satisfaction in doing these things correctly, from the certainty of getting no commendation.

"The great chance, also, of being censured, even in those cases where we had laboured most industriously to merit approbation, broke the spring of all generous exertion, and by teaching us to anticipate blame as a matter of course, defeated the very purpose of punishment when it fell upon us. The case being quite hopeless, the chastisement seldom conduced either to the amendment of an offender, or to the prevention of offences. But what seemed the oddest thing of all was, that these men were both as kind-hearted as could be; or, if there were any difference, the fault-finder was the better-natured, and, in matters not professional, the more indulgent of the two.

"The line of conduct I have described was purely a matter of official system, not at all of feeling. Yet, as it then appeared, and still appears to me, nothing could be more completely erroneous than the snarling method of the one, or more decidedly calculated to do good than the approving style of the other. It has, in fact, always appeared to me an absurdity, to make any real distinction between public and private matters in these respects.

"Nor is there the smallest reason why the same principle of civility, or consideration, or by whatever name that quality be called, by which the feelings of others are consulted, should not modify professional intercourse quite as much as it does that of the freest society, without any risk that the requisite strictness of discipline would be hurt by an attention to good manners.

"The desire of discovering that things are right, and a sincere wish to express our approbation, are habits which, in almost every situation in life, have the best possible effects in practice.

"They are vastly more agreeable certainly to the superior himself, whether he be the colonel of a regiment, the captain of a ship, or the head of a house; for the mere act of approving seldom fails to put a man's thoughts into that pleasant train which predisposes him to be habitually pleased, and this frame of mind alone, essentially helps the propagation of a similar cheerfulness among all those who are about him. It requires, indeed, but a very little experience of soldiers or sailors, children, servants, or any other kind of dependants, or even of companions and superiors, to show that this good-humour, on the part of those whom we wish to influence, is the best possible coadjutor to our schemes of management, whatever these may be."

The judicious bestowal of approbation is of the first importance in promoting obedience, and in cultivating in the bosom of your child affectionate and cheerful feelings. Let your smiles animate your boy's heart, and cheer him on in duty. When he returns from school, with his clothes clean and his countenance happy, reward him with the manifestation of a mother's love. This will be the strongest incentive to neatness and care. An English gentleman used to encourage his little children to early rising, by calling the one who first made her appearance in the parlour in the morning, Lark. The early riser was addressed by that name during the day. This slight expression of parental approval was found sufficient to call up all the children to the early enjoyment of the morning air. A child often makes a very great effort to do something to merit a smile from its mother. And most bitter tears are frequently shed because parents do not sufficiently sympathize in these feelings.

THE PECUNIARY INDEPENDENCE OF CHILDREN

CHILDREN should be early taught the value of money. In order to do this, they should be allowed the free use of a small sum, varying according to their age and the ability of their parents. This should never be given to them, but they should be allowed some means of *earning* it for themselves, and they should be taught to keep an accurate account of whatever they spend. If this practice were adopted, there would be fewer spendthrift sons and daughters to squander the hard earnings of their parents in useless extravagance, and then sink into poverty and want. They should early learn the relation between labour and its results, and their right of property be held as sacred as that of their seniors, lest their sense of justice be wounded by seeing that which they have regarded as their own, unceremoniously transferred to another without their consent. Said a young man of my acquaintance, " I remember the first dime I ever possessed. It was given me by a friend of my father's, who was visiting at our house, in return for attentions bestowed upon his horse. It was a proud and happy moment for me, and I could not refrain from showing my treasure to all who came in my way. My father, after looking at the shining coin for a moment, deliberately placed it *in his own* pocket, and it was lost to me for ever." Is it strange that the sons of such a father should become tenants of a jail before they arrive to manhood! Their rights have been outraged, and they have been deliberately taught a lesson of dishonesty. Nor are instances of this nature uncommon. Parents often, perhaps unconsciously, violate the sense of justice implanted in the breast of the child. A pet lamb is given them to train, or perhaps a calf or colt is called theirs, but when the animal is sold, they shed bitter tears over what is to them a loss of property. As a remedy for this, call nothing theirs which is not so in reality, and allow every child some means of earning a trifle which shall be their own, and you will cultivate a spirit of manly independence friendly to the growth of every virtue.

EXCITING IMAGINARY FEARS.

We extract the following from Mr. Abbott's "Mother at Home:"—

There is something very remarkable in the universal prevalence of superstition. Hardly an individual is to be found, enlightened or unenlightened, who is not, in a greater or less degree, under the influence of these irrational fears. There is, in the very nature of man, a strong susceptibility of impression upon this subject. A ghost story will be listened to with an intensity of interest which hardly anything else can awaken. Persons having the care of children, not unfrequently take advantage of this, and endeavour to amuse them by relating these stories, or to govern them by exciting their fears. It surely is not necessary to argue the impropriety of such a course. Every one knows how ruinous must be the result. Few parents, however, practise the caution which is necessary to prevent others from filling the minds of their children with superstition. How often do we find persons who retain through life the influence which has thus been exerted upon them in childhood! It becomes to them a real calamity. Much watchfulness is required to preserve the mind from such injuries.

There is a mode of punishment, not unfrequent, which is very reprehensible. A child is shut up in the cellar, or in a dark closet. It is thus led to associate ideas of terror with darkness. This effect has sometimes been so powerful, that hardly any motive would induce a child to go alone into a dark room. And sometimes even they fear, after they have retired for sleep, to be left alone without a light. But there is no difficulty in training up children to be as fearless by night as by day. And you can find many who do not even dream of danger in going anywhere about the house in the darkest night. If you would cultivate this state of mind in your children, it is necessary that you should preserve them from ideas of supernatural appearances, and should never appeal to imaginary fears. Train up your children to be virtuous and fearless. Moral courage is one of the surest safeguards of virtue.

An English writer gives a most appalling account of two instances in which fatal consequences attended the strong excitement of fear. Says he, "I knew in Philadelphia, as fine, and as sprightly, and as intelligent a child as ever was born, made an idiot for life, by being, when about three years old, shut into a dark closet by a maid-servant, in order to terrify it into silence. The thoughtless creature first menaced it with sending it to '*the bad place,*' and at last to reduce it to silence, put it into the closet, shut the door, and went out of the room. She went back in a few minutes, and found the child in a *fit*. It recovered from that, but was for life an idiot. When the parents, who had been out two days and two nights on a visit of pleasure, came home, they were told that the child had had *a fit*, but they were not told the cause. The girl, however, who was a neighbour's daughter, being on her death-bed about ten years afterward, could not die in peace without sending for the mother of the child and asking forgiveness of her. Thousands upon thousands of human beings have been deprived of their senses by these and similar means.

"It is not long since that we read, in the newspapers, of a child being absolutely *killed*—the case occurred at Birmingham, I think—by being thus frightened. The parents had gone out into what is called an evening party. The servants, naturally enough, had their party at home; and the mistress, who, by some unexpected accident, had been brought home at an early hour, finding the parlour full of company, ran up stairs to find her child, which was about two or three years old. She found it with its eyes open, but *fixed;* touching it, she found it inanimate. The doctor was sent for in vain: it was dead. The maid affected to know nothing of the cause; but some one of the parties assembled discovered, pinned up to the curtains of the bed. *a horrid figure*, made up partly of a frightful mask! This as the wretched girl confessed, had been done to keep the child *quiet* while she was with her company below. When one reflects on the anguish that the poor little thing must have endured before the life was quite frightened out of it, one can find no terms sufficiently strong to express the abhorrence due to the perpetrator of this crime, which was, in fact, a cruel murder; and, if it was beyond the reach of the law, it was so, because, as in the case of parricide, the law in making no provision for wickedness so unnatural, has, out of respect to human nature, supposed such crimes to be *impossible.*"

CHILD-TALK.

THE editor of the Musical World thus vindicates child-talk:—

Listen to the mother, talking comfort to her young babe. The comfort is surely not in the words—for the child understands not one of them. It lies, of course, then, in the music of the words. It is the mother's tone of voice—*her music*—which the child understands and receives into its little troubled heart.

I was lately one of a circle of friends where the conversation turned upon the prevailing manner of talking with very young children. One friend insisted strongly that mothers should talk common sense to their offspring; that it was just as intelligible, and in far better taste than nonsense; in short, that all this so-called baby-talk was as unnecessary as it was foolish.

Now, common sense is a very excellent thing; but— let us not overlook the *occasional uses of nonsense.* The truth is as I have already stated, very young children understand neither sense nor nonsense. They only *feel.* But the words they cannot feel—not comprehending them: it is of course, then, the music of the voice- -if they feel at all. Music, and particularly a mother's music, is the very language of feeling; and it is a " mother-tongue" perfectly well understood by the youngest child.

If a mother, for instance, is reproving a child, be the child ever so young, the reproof seems perfectly well understood; and we see its little watchful eye fixed steadily on the face of its mother. If cheering or enlivening, or frolicking, the child seems equally to understand what is meant. And here, again, it is the *tone* of cheerfulness, and the tone of reproof, and the tone of playfulness which is understood—not the word.

Does it not naturally follow, then, that the talking of plain common sense to such young children would be wholly impracticable, just for this reason—that we should fall inevitably *into the common-sense tone of voice;* which is the even and less musical voice of ordinary conversation—the voice of the intellect, not the voice of the heart? We should compose no pleasant music to what we were saying. Children, therefore, would not understand us. And though it might seem to us sound common sense enough, it might haply appear to the children great nonsense—for they would not understand, nor would they long to listen to us.

Let any mother try the experiment, and make a very sensible remark to her child, with the sensible tone of voice thereto appertaining; and see what degree of success that remark will have with her child.

We contended, therefore, with our disputing friends, that a mother's talk with her young child should be left, in all its naturalness and loving significance, e'en as it is—without the modern improvements. The motherly instinct is as beautiful as it is inevitable; and in no case is it more beautiful and truthful than is shown in her using a language with her child which it will understand —the language of music. The words are nothing; and they go for nothing. They serve merely as a means of articulation; and this is all the mother means by them. The music is not set to the words; but the words were simply used as syllables for the music. And, if listening, grown-up persons (for whom, albeit, the conversation is not intended) quarrel with the language of a mother in sweet communing with her child, let them close their intellect and *open their hearts* to the frequently irresistible charm of such motherly melody— and they will be content.

TEACH YOUR CHILDREN FROM THE BIBLE.

Mrs. M. T. Richards makes these good suggestions to mothers:—

All who have had the care of children are aware that they early need some kind of mental aliment. Such knowledge as they may gain by the senses of the various objects by which they are surrounded, first supplies this necessity. But the human mind ever grasping even in earliest childhood soon requires more, and an additional supply is furnished by the act of vividly conceiving and revolving the various ideas and images it has previously treasured.

Hence arises the delight of play. The little girl so intently engaged with her doll, is experiencing a delight purely mental. She moves in an entirely imaginary sphere, a little world of her own. She is busily conceiving and assuming the cares and anxieties of the mother, and at the same time transferring to her flaxen-haired treasure, the various peculiarities of childhood with a strength and vividness which to her mind has all the charm of reality.

The desire for stories which every mother knows is so universal and insatiable, springs from the same source. The pleasure which the child derives from these stories lies in the mental activity awakened by vividly conceiving of the subjects and events narrated to him. The imaginary "Henry" or "Willie," to whose sayings and doings he has so often been an eager listener, becomes a frequent companion of his thoughts, the hero of a drama, whose shifting scenes are often busily enacted in his mind. It will be found that the conceptive faculty thus exercised, as says Isaac Taylor, is one that is earliest developed, and is continually at work in childhood. With this, therefore, lies the very commencement of the process of intellectual training; and the result to be secured, that of giving scope and vigour to its action, affects most materially and permanently the whole mental character.

It is the work of the mother to supply the requisite material for the active and healthful exercise of the conceptive faculty. Her resources for this are abundant: descriptions of scenes or events which her child may or may not have witnessed; sketches, even the rudest outlines of animals, trees, or any tangible object, and what is usually most called for, and most available, narrations of individual characters, known as "stories."

Now it is here we would plead the excellence of the Bible, as affording to the mother an unfailing treasury, whence she may draw continually, without fear of exhausting her resources. It is true that the materials for stories are as multiplied and various as the scenes and incidents of every day life, but aside from all these, and above them all, are the tales which may be told from the Bible. There is in them a life, a truthfulness, a graphic power which will ever remain unequalled. They pass before the child's mind as pictures of life and beauty, and leave their impress indelibly engraven thereon. Let the offering up of Isaac be narrated, and as the tale advances, the flushed cheek and mouth half-parted in suspense, the clasped hands as if in supplication, as the fatal blow is about to be struck, and the joy lighting up the countenance as the forbidding voice is heard from heaven, strongly testify how vividly the whole is conceived, how life-like is the scene transpiring before the mental vision. Tell of the shining ladder, with the angels of God ascending and descending upon it. Paint the scene where the sleeping babe lay cradled upon the banks of the Nile. Unroll the gorgeous panorama of the history of Joseph. Show the waters of the Red Sea forming a wall on the right hand and on the left; the manna; the flowing rock; the burning quaking mount, with the whole multitude retreating in terror afar off, and Moses "drawing near unto the thick darkness where God was," and the mind of the child is furnished with subjects of conception and thought which could be derived from no other source. The marvellousness of the Scripture records casts its wondrous spell over his whole being, enchaining every faculty to their contemplation. His thoughts become accustomed to stretch beyond the line of his outward vision. His conceptions take hold on things untried and strange. And he is thus acquiring a breadth and amplitude of capacity which will yet stamp its decided impress upon his future mental character.

Let the mother then become a diligent student of the Scriptures, that she may be "thoroughly furnished" with Bible stories for the instruction of her child. The advantage she may thus impart to him will be threefold: it will induce a mental activity; it will provide a select supply of intellectual furniture as it were, which the mind is storing for constant use; and it will give the renowned characters of sacred lore a hold upon his veneration and love, which the lapse of years shall rarely be able to displace. All this may be done for young children, but as they advance through the later periods of childhood to youth, the Bible may still be the mother's grand text-book in their instruction.

PUNISHMENT.

THERE is probably no duty which the mother is called to perform, so trying to her feelings, as the infliction of punishment. And many a one, shrinking from the duty, when the first grave offence of her child demanded it at her hands, has multiplied tenfold its subsequent necessity. We have known cases, in which a signal punishment for a child's first falsehood, has been sufficient for a lifetime, and a character of beautiful veracity has been henceforth established. And instances will occur to every one, in which the omission of this punishment has perpetuated the sin of lying, till it became a settled habit, destroying all confidence in the character so ruinously neglected.

It will greatly increase the moral power of punishment in any given instance, if the child can be made to feel and acknowledge its justice. The punishment of David for causing the death of Uriah presents a forcible illustration of this point. By the parable of the prophet his sin was pictured vividly before him, in its real deformity and guilt. He looked steadily at it, unveiled by the distorting mists of prejudice, unprotected by the invulnerable shield of selfishness And when the prophet fastened the king's unqualified condemnation of so aggravated a crime upon his own head, he had not a word to offer in extenuation or self-defence. The mother may often adopt this method of making her child perceive his guilt. Let him look at his sin as he would regard it in another, and she thus divests it of many of the excuses and palliations which his self-love has thrown around it.

Let not then the mother, as she values the present and future welfare of her child, weakly shrink from this painful duty, but faithfully meet it when first demanded, and she may be assured that she will be called but seldom to its discharge; and if she be tempted to feel that *one* deliberate falsehood, in a child habitually truthful, may be passed by, or *one* act of wilful disobedience, in a child usually docile, may be disregarded, let her remember Moses, who by his usually quiet and forbearing spirit, gained the appellation of the "meekest man," yet for one act of anger was forbidden to enter the land of promise.

THOUGHTS FOR MOTHERS.

THE influence which woman exerts is silent and still, felt rather than seen, not chaining the hands, but restraining our actions by gliding into the heart.

Young children often do wrong merely from the immaturity of their reason, or from a mistaken principle; and when this is the case, they should be tenderly reproved, and patiently shown their error.

The real object of education is to give children resources that will endure as long as life endures; habits that will ameliorate, not destroy; occupations that will render sickness tolerable, solitude pleasant, age venerable, life more dignified and useful, and death less terrible.

Do all in your power to teach your children self-government. If a child is passionate, teach him by gentle and patient means to curb his temper. If he is greedy, cultivate liberality in him. If he is selfish, promote generosity. If he is sulky, charm him out of it, by encouraging frank good-humour. If he is indolent, accustom him to exertion, and train him so as to perform even onerous duties with alacrity. If pride comes in to make his obedience reluctant, subdue him, either by counsel or discipline. In short, give your children the habit of overcoming their besetting sins.

HEALTH OF CHILDREN.

More than half the diseases from which children suffer, are caused by the injudicious treatment they receive at the hands of those who can have no excuse for their ignorance. The influence of the brain on the digestive organs is direct. During childhood, when the brain is, in common with other organs, in a state of great activity and rapid development, the proper arrangement of diet is of the greatest importance. Cheerful activity, cleanliness, dry pure air, adequate clothing, and a suitable regimen, are indispensable promoters of health. Horses and cattle are carefully fed with the food that suits them best; and by humane people greater care is bestowed upon them than the majority of parents give to their children. Some may think we are colouring too highly this state of things; that all right-minded parents love their children too much willingly to injure them. Still we may kill them by misguided kindness. Look into society, as it is at present constituted, and your own knowledge will furnish you with instances of grievous wrong done to children by parents violating the physical laws of their being. We know many such and we do not hesitate to say it, for such is our conviction, that if their children be not removed when young from the deteriorating example and pernicious training of their parents, they will in all probability become gluttons and drunkards. High-seasoned and unwholesome food is given in such large quantities, and at such irregular times, that unnatural appetites are created, and digestion impaired. Stimulating and poisonous substances are administered to them to invigorate their systems, which have quite the contrary effect, and lay the foundation for all kinds of maladies in future years. Some mothers so stuff their children the whole year round with unwholesome, exciting, and stimulating meats and drinks, that they become complete gourmands, and their whole thoughts are occupied with what they shall eat, what they shall drink, and wherewithal they shall be clothed. If parents would give their children good, wholesome, nourishing food, their only drink water, and let strict regularity and punctuality be observed in regard to their times of eating, a gradual change for the better would distinctly mark the rising generation; for it is most certain that parents cannot be too particular about the dietetic habits of their children. Their happiness here and hereafter greatly depend upon the right physiological training or treatment given them in early life. And yet how many mothers make their table a snare to their offspring by pampering their appetites, and loading their stomachs with improper food!

THE END.

www.ingramcontent.com/pod-product-compliance
Lightning Source LLC
Chambersburg PA
CBHW021955220426
43663CB00007B/818